AMERICAN FO[

A Comprehensive Guide

Marcus B. Cole

Table of Contents

Get A Free Book At: xspurts.com/posts/free-book-offer[4]

5

---

1. https://Xspurts.com

2. https://Xspurts.com

3. https://Xspurts.com

4. https://xspurts.com/posts/free-book-offer

5. https://xspurts.com/

History of American Football

American football is a popular sport that has been played in the United States for well over a century. The sport is known for its physicality, strategy, and athleticism, and has captured the attention of millions of people across the country. Below we will we will explore the history of American football, from its origins in the late 19th century to the present day.

Origins of American Football

The origins of American football can be traced back to several different sports, including rugby and soccer. In the mid-19th century, these sports were popular in the United States, but they were often played under different rules depending on the region of the country. The first game of American football was played on November 6, 1869, between Rutgers and Princeton. The game was played using rules that were based on those of rugby, but it also incorporated elements of soccer and other sports.

Over the next several decades, American football continued to evolve as a sport. In 1880, Walter Camp, a student at Yale, helped to develop a set of rules that would standardize the game and make it more structured. These rules included the use of a line of scrimmage, downs, and a scoring system that awarded points for touchdowns, field goals, and safeties.

Early Years of American Football

During the early years of American football, the sport was primarily played by college teams. However, it quickly gained popularity, and by the early 20th century, it had become a professional sport. The first professional football league, the Ohio League, was formed in 1903, and it was followed by the formation of other leagues, including the National Football League (NFL) in 1920.

One of the most significant events in the early history of American football was the introduction of the forward pass. Prior to the introduction of the forward pass, the game was primarily played using running plays, which often resulted in a scrum of players fighting for the ball. In 1906, the forward pass was legalized, which allowed quarterbacks to throw the ball downfield to receivers. This change in the rules opened up the game and made it more exciting for fans.

Golden Age of American Football

The 1920s and 1930s are often referred to as the "Golden Age" of American football. During this time, the sport continued to grow in popularity, and many of the traditions that are still a part of the game today were established. One of the most significant events of this time was the creation of the NFL Championship game, which was first played in 1933. This game would later become known as the Super Bowl.

During this time, many of the greatest players in the history of the sport emerged. Players like Red Grange, Jim Thorpe, and Bronko Nagurski became household names, and they helped to establish the sport as a major form of entertainment in the United States. The popularity of American football was also aided by the rise of radio and television, which allowed fans to follow their favorite teams and players from anywhere in the country.

Post-World War II Era

The post-World War II era was a time of tremendous growth for American football. The sport had become firmly established as a major form of entertainment, and the NFL had become the dominant professional league. During this time, many of the traditions that are still a part of the game today were established, including the use of helmets, face masks, and shoulder pads.

One of the most significant events of this era was the emergence of the West Coast offense. This offensive system, which was developed by coaches like Bill Walsh and Don Coryell, emphasized the use of short, quick passes and was designed to take advantage of the speed and agility of smaller players.

Origins and early development

American football is a uniquely American sport, and its origins can be traced back to a variety of different sources. Some of the earliest forms of football were played in Europe in the 1800s, but the modern game of American football was developed in the United States in the late 19th and early 20th centuries.

One of the earliest forms of football was a game played in England called rugby. This game was played with a round ball, and players would run with the ball and try to score by crossing the opponent's goal line. The game was popular among college students in England, and it eventually made its way to the United States in the mid-1800s.

In the United States, the game of rugby was adapted to create a new game called American football. The first game of American football was played on November 6, 1869, between Princeton and Rutgers. The game was played with a round ball and had many similarities to rugby.

Over time, American football began to evolve and develop its own unique set of rules and strategies. One of the key innovations in the early development of American football was the introduction of the oval-shaped ball, which made it easier to throw and catch.

In the early days of American football, the game was primarily played by college students. The rules were still evolving, and there was a great deal of variation in how the game was played from one school to the next. One of the key figures in the early development of American football was Walter Camp, who is often referred to as the "father of American football." Camp was a football player and coach who helped to standardize the rules of the game and make it more structured.

In 1880, Camp proposed a set of rules that would become the basis for modern American football. These rules included the introduction of the line of scrimmage and the down-and-distance system, which made the game more organized and strategic. The line of scrimmage is the point on the field where the ball is placed before each play, and the down-and-distance system requires the offense to advance the ball a certain number of yards in a set number of plays.

Another key innovation in the early development of American football was the introduction of the forward pass. In the early days of the game, the ball could only be advanced by running with it or kicking it. However, in 1906, the rules were changed to allow the quarterback to throw the ball forward, which opened up new possibilities for offensive strategy.

In the early 1900s, American football began to gain popularity beyond college campuses. Professional football leagues were established, and the game became a popular spectator sport. The National Football League (NFL) was founded in 1920, and it quickly became the premier professional football league in the United States.

Throughout the early development of American football, the game continued to evolve and change. New strategies and techniques were developed, and the rules were refined to make the game more exciting and competitive. Today, American football is one of the most popular sports in the United States, and it continues to evolve and change with each passing season.

In conclusion, American football has a rich and complex history that spans more than a century. The game was influenced by a variety of different sources, including rugby and other early forms of football. The early development of American football was marked by a great deal of experimentation and variation, but over time, the game became more structured and organized. Today, American football is a beloved sport that is enjoyed by millions of people around the world, and its origins and early development continue to fascinate football fans and historians alike.

Evolution of rules and gameplay

American football is a uniquely American sport, and its origins can be traced back to a variety of different sources. Some of the earliest forms of football were played in Europe in the 1800s, but the modern game of American football was developed in the United States in the late 19th and early 20th centuries.

One of the earliest forms of football was a game played in England called rugby. This game was played with a round ball, and players would run with the ball and try to score by crossing the opponent's goal line. The game was popular among college students in England, and it eventually made its way to the United States in the mid-1800s.

In the United States, the game of rugby was adapted to create a new game called American football. The first game of American football was played on November 6, 1869, between Princeton and Rutgers. The game was played with a round ball and had many similarities to rugby.

Over time, American football began to evolve and develop its own unique set of rules and strategies. One of the key innovations in the early development of American football was the introduction of the oval-shaped ball, which made it easier to throw and catch.

In the early days of American football, the game was primarily played by college students. The rules were still evolving, and there was a great deal of variation in how the game was played from one school to the next. One of the key figures in the early development of American football was Walter Camp, who is often referred to as the "father of American football." Camp was a football player and coach who helped to standardize the rules of the game and make it more structured.

In 1880, Camp proposed a set of rules that would become the basis for modern American football. These rules included the introduction of the line of scrimmage and the down-and-distance system, which made the game more organized and strategic. The line of scrimmage is the point on the field where the ball is placed before each play, and the down-and-distance system requires the offense to advance the ball a certain number of yards in a set number of plays.

Another key innovation in the early development of American football was the introduction of the forward pass. In the early days of the game, the ball could only be advanced by running with it or kicking it. However, in 1906, the rules were changed to allow the quarterback to throw the ball forward, which opened up new possibilities for offensive strategy.

In the early 1900s, American football began to gain popularity beyond college campuses. Professional football leagues were established, and the game became a popular spectator sport. The National Football League (NFL) was founded in 1920, and it quickly became the premier professional football league in the United States.

Throughout the early development of American football, the game continued to evolve and change. New strategies and techniques were developed, and the rules were refined to make the game more exciting and competitive. Today, American football is one of the most popular sports in the United States, and it continues to evolve and change with each passing season.

In conclusion, American football has a rich and complex history that spans more than a century. The game was influenced by a variety of different sources, including rugby and other early forms of football. The early development of American football was marked by a great deal of experimentation and variation, but over time, the game became more structured and organized. Today, American football is a beloved sport that is enjoyed by millions of people around the world, and its origins and early development continue to fascinate football fans and historians alike.

Growth of professional and college football

Football is one of the most popular sports in the United States, and it has a rich history that spans over a century. The sport has undergone many changes and evolutions over the years, and it has grown to become a major form of entertainment for millions of people across the country. Below we will we will explore the growth of professional and college football, from its early days to the present day.

Early Days of Football

Football has its roots in rugby, which was a popular sport in the United States in the late 19th century. The first game of American football was played in 1869, between Rutgers and Princeton, and it was played using rules that were based on those of rugby. Over time, American football began to evolve and develop its own unique rules and style of play.

During the early days of football, the sport was primarily played by college teams. However, it quickly gained popularity, and by the early 20th century, it had become a professional sport. The first professional football league, the Ohio League, was formed in 1903, and it was followed by the formation of other leagues, including the National Football League (NFL) in 1920.

Growth of Professional Football

The growth of professional football in the United States was slow but steady. During the early days of the NFL, the league struggled to attract fans and to generate revenue. However, this began to change in the 1950s and 1960s, as the NFL began to invest in marketing and television coverage.

One of the most significant events in the growth of professional football was the introduction of the Super Bowl in 1967. The Super Bowl is the championship game of the NFL, and it is one of the most-watched television events in the United States. The Super Bowl helped to establish football as a major form of entertainment in the United States and helped to attract a larger audience to the sport.

Another significant event in the growth of professional football was the merger of the AFL and the NFL in 1970. The AFL was a rival league that had been formed in 1960, and it had established itself as a major force in professional football. The merger of the two leagues helped to create a more competitive and exciting product, and it helped to establish the NFL as the dominant professional football league in the United States.

Growth of College Football

College football has also undergone significant growth and evolution over the years. The sport has a long and rich history, and it has been played at colleges and universities across the country for well over a century.

One of the most significant events in the growth of college football was the establishment of the NCAA in 1906. The NCAA is the governing body for college athletics in the United States, and it helped to establish rules and regulations for college football that helped to make the sport more structured and organized.

Over the years, college football has grown to become a major form of entertainment in the United States. The sport is known for its pageantry and traditions, and it attracts millions of fans to stadiums across the country each year.

One of the most significant events in the growth of college football was the establishment of the Bowl Championship Series (BCS) in 1998. The BCS was a system that was used to determine the national champion in college football, and it helped to establish a more competitive and exciting product. The BCS was replaced by the College Football Playoff in 2014, which is a four-team playoff that is used to determine the national champion.

Understanding the Game

Understanding the game of American football is essential for players, coaches, and spectators alike. The game is full of complex rules, strategies, and terminology, which can be daunting for those who are new to the sport. In this article, we will discuss the fundamentals of American football, including the rules, positions, and basic strategies.

The Basics of American Football

American football is played with two teams of 11 players each. The game is divided into four quarters, each lasting 15 minutes. At the beginning of each half and after every score, the ball is kicked off to the other team. The team with possession of the ball is known as the offense, while the team without possession is known as the defense.

The objective of the game is for the offense to advance the ball down the field and score points by crossing the opponent's goal line or kicking the ball through the opponent's goalposts. The defense's objective is to prevent the offense from scoring and to gain possession of the ball.

The game is played on a rectangular field that measures 120 yards in length and 53.3 yards in width. The playing field is divided into two halves by a midfield line, and each half is further divided into two 30-yard long end zones. The offense must advance the ball into the opponent's end zone to score a touchdown, which is worth six points. The team can also score points by kicking the ball through the opponent's goalposts, which is known as a field goal and is worth three points.

The offense has four downs, or attempts, to advance the ball 10 yards. If the offense is successful in advancing the ball 10 yards, they are given a new set of downs to continue the drive. If they fail to advance the ball 10 yards in four downs, possession of the ball is turned over to the defense.

The Positions in American Football

There are several positions in American football, each with its own unique set of responsibilities.

Quarterback: The quarterback is the leader of the offense and is responsible for throwing the ball and directing the offense. The quarterback takes the ball from the center, either by hand or by a snap, and then makes a decision to either pass the ball to a receiver or hand it off to a running back.

Running Back: The running back is responsible for carrying the ball and gaining yards. They can also catch passes from the quarterback.

Wide Receiver: The wide receiver is responsible for catching passes from the quarterback and gaining yards. They typically line up on the outside of the offensive formation.

Tight End: The tight end is a hybrid position that can block like an offensive lineman or catch passes like a receiver. They typically line up on the offensive line.

Offensive Linemen: The offensive linemen are responsible for blocking the defense and creating running lanes for the running back. There are five offensive linemen, including a center who snaps the ball to the quarterback.

Defensive Linemen: The defensive linemen are responsible for stopping the offense from advancing the ball. They typically line up on the defensive line.

Linebackers: The linebackers are responsible for stopping the running back and covering receivers in the middle of the field.

Defensive Backs: The defensive backs are responsible for covering the receivers and preventing them from catching passes.

Understanding Basic Strategies in American Football

There are several basic strategies in American football that teams use to gain an advantage over their opponents.

Offense: The offense's primary strategy is to move the ball down the field and score points. They can do this through passing the ball, running the ball, or a combination of both. The offense will typically use a variety of plays to keep the defense guessing, including running plays, passing plays, and trick plays.

Defense: The defense's primary strategy is to prevent the offense from scoring points. They can do this by stopping the running back, covering the receivers, and pressuring the quarterback. The defense will typically use a variety of formations and strategies to confuse the offense and disrupt their plays.

Special Teams: Special teams are responsible for kickoffs, punts, and field goals. They can also score points through a punt or kickoff return. The special teams' primary strategy is to create field position for the offense and prevent the opposing team from scoring.

Conclusion

Understanding the game of American football is essential for players, coaches, and spectators alike. The game is full of complex rules, strategies, and terminology, which can be daunting for those who are new to the sport. By understanding the basics of American football, including the rules, positions, and basic strategies, individuals can fully appreciate the excitement and intensity of this great American pastime.

Objectives and scoring

Objectives and scoring are integral components of American football. The game is played with the objective of scoring points by advancing the ball across the opponent's goal line or kicking the ball through the opponent's goalposts. The team with the highest score at the end of the game is declared the winner.

There are several ways to score points in American football. The most common methods are touchdowns, field goals, extra points, and two-point conversions.

A touchdown is scored when a player carrying the ball crosses the opponent's goal line or catches a pass in the end zone. A touchdown is worth six points, and the scoring team is given the opportunity to score an extra point or two-point conversion.

A field goal is scored when the ball is kicked through the opponent's goalposts. A field goal is worth three points and can be attempted from anywhere on the field.

After scoring a touchdown, the scoring team has the option of attempting an extra point or two-point conversion. An extra point is a kick attempt from the opponent's two-yard line and is worth one point. A two-point conversion is a play attempt from the opponent's two-yard line and is worth two points.

In addition to these primary methods of scoring, there are also several ways to score points through defensive plays. For example, if the defense tackles the offensive player with the ball in their own end zone, the defense is awarded two points. This is known as a safety.

Another way that the defense can score points is by intercepting a pass thrown by the opposing team and returning it for a touchdown. This is worth six points and is known as a pick-six.

Understanding the scoring system is important for players, coaches, and spectators. It helps players to understand the value of each play and to strategize their game plan accordingly. Coaches use the scoring system to design plays and strategies that maximize their team's chances of scoring points. Spectators use the scoring system to follow the game and to celebrate their team's successes.

In addition to the primary methods of scoring, there are also several strategies that teams use to gain an advantage over their opponents. One such strategy is the use of the two-minute drill. This is a play-calling strategy that is used when a team is trailing in the final minutes of the game. The goal of the two-minute drill is to move the ball quickly down the field and score a touchdown or field goal before time runs out.

Another strategy that teams use is the use of trick plays. Trick plays are designed to deceive the opposing team and create scoring opportunities. For example, a fake punt is a play where the punter appears to be punting the ball but instead throws a pass to a receiver for a first down.

The scoring system and objectives of American football have evolved over time. The game was originally played with a different set of rules, and scoring was much more difficult. For example, in the early days of American football, touchdowns were only worth four points, and field goals were worth five points.

Over time, the game has become more focused on scoring, and the rules have been updated to reflect this. The addition of the two-point conversion and the extra point kick has made scoring more dynamic and exciting.

In conclusion, objectives and scoring are essential components of American football. The game is played with the objective of scoring points by advancing the ball across the opponent's goal line or kicking the ball through the opponent's goalposts. Understanding the scoring system is important for players, coaches, and spectators alike. It helps players to understand the value of each play and to strategize their game plan accordingly. Coaches use the scoring system to design plays and strategies that maximize their team's chances of scoring points, while spectators use the scoring system to follow the game and celebrate their team's successes. Overall, the scoring system and objectives of American football make it one of the most exciting and dynamic sports in the world.

Field dimensions and markings

Field dimensions and markings are essential components of American football. The field is rectangular and measures 120 yards in length and 53.3 yards in width. It is divided into two halves, each measuring 60 yards in length, and separated by a midfield line. The midfield line is marked with an arrowhead that points towards the end zone of the team that is set to receive the ball on the opening kickoff.

The width of the field is marked with two white lines that run parallel to the length of the field. These lines are known as the sidelines, and they are located 10 yards from each sideline. The area between the sidelines is the playing field and is further divided into five-yard increments by hash marks that run perpendicular to the sidelines.

At each end of the field is an end zone, which is 10 yards deep and 53.3 yards wide. The end zones are marked with a solid white line extending from one sideline to the other. The goal line is the line that marks the front of the end zone, and it is also marked with a solid white line.

On either side of the field, there are two uprights that are 18 feet, 6 inches apart. These uprights are connected by a horizontal bar that is 10 feet above the ground. This structure is known as the goalpost, and it is used to determine whether a field goal or extra point is successful.

In addition to these basic dimensions and markings, there are several other markings on the field that are used to provide additional information to players, officials, and spectators. These include:

Yard lines: Every five yards on the field is marked with a line that runs perpendicular to the sidelines. These lines are numbered from zero to 50, with zero being the midfield line.

End line: The line that marks the back of the end zone is called the end line. It is also marked with a solid white line.

Sideline markers: At regular intervals along the sideline, there are markers that indicate the yard line. These markers are usually orange and are placed at the 20-yard line, 30-yard line, 40-yard line, and midfield.

Coaching boxes: Each team has a designated area on the sideline where coaches and other team personnel are allowed to stand during the game. These areas are marked with white lines and are located between the 25-yard line and the 10-yard line.

Hash marks: The hash marks are used to mark the location of the ball between plays. They are located in the middle of the field, and each hash mark is 70 feet, 9 inches from the nearest sideline.

Inbounds lines: Along the sidelines, there are lines that mark the area where the ball must be placed for the next play to be considered inbounds. These lines are usually two yards from the sideline, and they are marked with small white circles.

Goal line pylons: At each corner of the end zone, there is a pylon that marks the location of the goal line.

Penalty markers: When a penalty is called, the official will place a marker on the field to indicate where the penalty occurred. These markers are usually bright orange and are placed at the spot of the foul.

Understanding the dimensions and markings of the field is essential for players, coaches, and officials. It helps players to understand where they are on the field and what they need to do to advance the ball. Coaches can use the markings to design plays and strategies that take advantage of the field's layout. Officials use the markings to determine whether a play is legal or illegal and to mark the location of penalties.

In addition to the markings on the field, there are also rules governing how the field should be maintained. For example, the grass should be cut to a height of no more than two inches, and any divots or holes should be filled in before the game. The field should also be level and free from any hazards that could cause injury to players.

In conclusion, the dimensions and markings of the field are an essential part of American football. They provide players, coaches, and officials with the information they need to understand the game and make informed decisions. Understanding these markings is essential for anyone who wants to learn or play American football, and it is an important part of the game's rich history and tradition.

Key terms and jargon

- End zone - the area at each end of the field where touchdowns are scored
- Down - a single play in football
- First down - the first in a set of four downs to advance the ball ten yards
- Line of scrimmage - an imaginary line where the ball is placed at the start of each play
- Snap - the act of the center passing the ball to the quarterback to start a play
- Quarterback - the player who leads the offense and throws the ball
- Running back - the player who runs with the ball
- Wide receiver - the player who catches passes thrown by the quarterback
- Tight end - a player who lines up on the offensive line and can catch passes
- Offensive line - the players who block for the quarterback

and running back

- Blitz - when a defensive player rushes the quarterback to try to sack him
- Sack - when a defensive player tackles the quarterback behind the line of scrimmage
- Interception - when a defensive player catches a pass thrown by the quarterback
- Fumble - when a player drops the ball while running or being tackled
- Touchdown - when the ball is carried or caught into the opponent's end zone
- Field goal - when the ball is kicked through the opponent's goalposts
- Extra point - a kick attempt after a touchdown for an additional point
- Two-point conversion - a play attempt after a touchdown, worth two points
- Offside - when a defensive player crosses the line of scrimmage before the snap
- False start - when an offensive player moves before the snap
- Holding - when an offensive player grabs a defensive player to prevent them from making a play
- Pass interference - when a defensive player interferes with a receiver's attempt to catch a pass
- Red zone - the area inside the opponent's 20-yard line
- Huddle - when the offensive players gather together to discuss the next play
- Shotgun formation - when the quarterback lines up a few yards behind the center to receive the snap
- Play action - when the quarterback fakes a handoff to a running back and then throws a pass
- Option - when the quarterback can choose to hand off the

ball to a running back or keep it and run himself

- Wildcat - a formation where a running back takes the snap instead of the quarterback
- Screen pass - a short pass to a receiver who is surrounded by blockers
- Draw play - a play where the quarterback drops back to pass, but hands off the ball to a running back instead
- Zone defense - a defensive strategy where each defender covers a specific area of the field
- Man-to-man defense - a defensive strategy where each defender is responsible for covering a specific offensive player
- Nickel defense - a defensive strategy where an extra defensive back is added to cover receivers
- Dime defense - a defensive strategy where two extra defensive backs are added to cover receivers
- Cover 2 defense - a defensive strategy where two safeties cover the deep part of the field
- Cover 3 defense - a defensive strategy where three defenders cover the deep part of the field
- Blitz pickup - when the offensive line blocks to protect the quarterback from a blitz
- Stunt - when defensive linemen switch positions to try to confuse the offensive line
- Zone read - a play where the quarterback reads the defense and decides whether to keep the ball or hand it off to a running back
- Play clock - the amount of time given to the offense to run a play before a penalty is called
- Challenge - when a coach challenges a call made by the officials on the field
- Instant replay - a video review of a play to determine

whether the call on the field was correct
- Overtime - an extra period of play in the event of a tie game
- Onside kick - a kick where the kicking team tries to recover the ball themselves
- Fair catch - when a receiver signals that they will not attempt to run after catching a punt or kickoff
- Touchback - when a kickoff or punt goes into the opponent's end zone and is not returned
- Punt return - when a player catches a punt and runs it back for a gain of yards
- Kickoff return - when a player catches a kickoff and runs it back for a gain of yards
- Punt block - when a defensive player tries to block a punt
- Field position - the location on the field where the ball is being played
- Pylon - a marker at each corner of the end zone
- Tackle - when a defensive player brings down an offensive player with the ball
- Safety - when the offense is tackled in their own end zone, resulting in two points for the defense
- Delay of game - when the offense takes too long to run a play, resulting in a penalty
- Tripping - when a player uses their leg to trip an opponent, resulting in a penalty
- Personal foul - a penalty for an unnecessary or dangerous hit or action
- Facemask - a penalty for grabbing an opponent's facemask
- Roughing the passer - a penalty for hitting the quarterback after they have thrown the ball
- Incomplete pass - when a pass is thrown and not caught by a receiver

- Pass rush - when the defensive line tries to get to the quarterback to disrupt a pass play.

Positions and Player Roles

American football is a complex and dynamic sport that requires a diverse range of skills and abilities. Each player on the field has a specific position and role to play, and understanding these positions and roles is essential for understanding the game. Below we will we will explore the positions and player roles in American football, including the rules and regulations that govern the sport.

Offensive Positions

1. Quarterback: The quarterback is the leader of the offense and is responsible for calling plays, throwing the ball, and making decisions on the field.

2. Running Back: The running back is responsible for carrying the ball and making runs up the field.

3. Wide Receiver: The wide receiver is responsible for catching passes from the quarterback and advancing the ball up the field.

4. Tight End: The tight end is a hybrid position that combines the skills of a receiver and a lineman. They are responsible for blocking and catching passes.

5. Offensive Lineman: The offensive lineman is responsible for blocking the defense and protecting the quarterback.

Defensive Positions

6. Defensive Lineman: The defensive lineman is responsible for stopping the run and putting pressure on the quarterback.

7. Linebacker: The linebacker is responsible for covering the middle of the field and stopping the run.

8. Cornerback: The cornerback is responsible for covering the wide receivers and preventing them from catching passes.

9. Safety: The safety is responsible for covering the deep part of the field and preventing long passes.

Special Teams Positions

10. Kicker: The kicker is responsible for kicking field goals and extra points.

11. Punter: The punter is responsible for punting the ball downfield and pinning the opposing team deep in their own territory.

12. Kick Returner: The kick returner is responsible for returning kickoffs and punts.

Player Roles

In addition to the specific positions on the field, each player has a specific role to play. These roles can vary depending on the situation and the strategy of the team. Some of the most common player roles in American football include:

13. Blockers: Players who are responsible for blocking the defense and creating holes for the running backs.

14. Pass Catchers: Players who are responsible for catching passes from the quarterback and advancing the ball up the field.

15. Pass Rushers: Players who are responsible for putting pressure on the quarterback and disrupting the opposing team's offense.

16. Tacklers: Players who are responsible for tackling the opposing team's ball carriers and preventing them from gaining yardage.

17. Coverage Players: Players who are responsible for covering the opposing team's receivers and preventing them from catching passes.

American football is a complex and dynamic sport that requires a diverse range of skills and abilities. Each player on the field has a specific position and role to play, and understanding these positions and roles is essential for understanding the game. By understanding the positions and player roles in American football, players and fans can better appreciate the strategy and excitement of this popular sport.

Special teams

American football is a complex and dynamic sport that requires a diverse range of skills and abilities. In addition to the offensive and defensive positions, each team also has special teams players who are responsible for the kicking and returning aspects of the game. Below we will we will explore the special teams in American football, including the rules and regulations that govern the sport.

Kickers

1. Kickers are responsible for kicking the ball off to start the game, kicking field goals, and kicking extra points after touchdowns. There are two types of kickers in American football: the placekicker and the punter.

Placekicker

The placekicker is responsible for kicking field goals and extra points. Field goals are worth three points, and extra points are worth one point. The placekicker must have excellent accuracy and leg strength to be successful in this position.

Punter

The punter is responsible for punting the ball to the opposing team after the offense fails to make a first down. The punter must have excellent leg strength and accuracy to pin the opposing team deep in their own territory.

Kick Returners

Kick returners are responsible for returning kickoffs and punts. They must have excellent speed, agility, and vision to avoid tackles and advance the ball up the field.

Special Teams Roles

In addition to the specific positions on special teams, each player has a specific role to play. These roles can vary depending on the situation and the strategy of the team. Some of the most common roles in special teams include:

2. Gunner: The gunner is responsible for covering punts and kickoffs and tackling the returner.

3. Long Snapper: The long snapper is responsible for snapping the ball to the punter or placekicker.

4. Holder: The holder is responsible for holding the ball for the placekicker on field goals and extra points.

5. Kickoff Specialist: The kickoff specialist is responsible for kicking the ball deep into the opposing team's territory on kickoffs.

6. Coverage Players: The coverage players are responsible for covering punts and kickoffs and preventing the opposing team from advancing the ball up the field.

Rules and Regulations

There are several rules and regulations that govern special teams in American football. Some of the most important rules include:

7. Fair Catch: A fair catch can be signaled by the returner by raising his hand above his head. Once a fair catch is signaled, the returner cannot be tackled, and the ball is placed at the spot of the catch.

8. Touchback: A touchback occurs when the ball is kicked into the end zone and is not returned. The ball is placed at the 20-yard line for the receiving team.

9. Onside Kick: An onside kick is a type of kickoff where the kicking team attempts to recover the ball immediately after it is kicked. Onside kicks can only be attempted once per half.

10. Blocking: Special teams players are allowed to block their opponents, but they cannot block from behind or below the waist.

11. Offside: Special teams players must line up behind the ball on kickoffs and punts. If a player is lined up in front of the ball when it is kicked, it is considered offside and results in a penalty.

Special teams are an essential part of American football and require a diverse range of skills and abilities. Kickers, kick returners, and special teams players all play important roles in the game, and understanding these roles is essential for understanding the sport. By understanding the special teams in American football, players and fans can better appreciate the strategy and excitement of this popular sport.

Basic Offensive Strategies

American football is a complex and dynamic sport that requires a diverse range of skills and abilities. One of the keys to success in American football is having a well-designed offensive strategy. Below we will we will explore some of the basic offensive strategies used in American football, including the different formations, plays, and tactics that teams use to score points.

Formations

The offensive formation is the way that the offensive players line up before the snap of the ball. There are many different types of formations used in American football, but some of the most common include:

1. I-Formation: The I-Formation is a traditional formation that features the quarterback under center, a fullback in front of the running back, and two wide receivers.

2. Shotgun Formation: The Shotgun Formation features the quarterback in the shotgun position, with a running back or tight end lined up next to him. This formation allows the quarterback to see the field better and have more time to throw the ball.

3. Spread Formation: The Spread Formation features the offense spreading out across the field, with multiple receivers and a single backfield player. This formation is designed to stretch the defense and create mismatches in coverage.

Plays

Once the formation is set, the offense will run a play to try and advance the ball up the field. There are many different types of plays used in American football, but some of the most common include:

4. Run Play: A run play is designed to hand the ball off to a running back and have him run up the field. The offensive line will block the defense to create holes for the running back to run through.

5. Pass Play: A pass play is designed to have the quarterback throw the ball to a receiver downfield. The offensive line will protect the quarterback from the defense and give him time to throw the ball.

6. Play-Action Pass: A play-action pass is designed to fake a run play and then have the quarterback throw the ball downfield. This play is designed to deceive the defense and create an opening for the receiver.

Tactics

In addition to formations and plays, the offense can use different tactics to gain an advantage over the defense. Some of the most common offensive tactics used in American football include:

7. Audibles: Audibles are changes in the play that the quarterback makes at the line of scrimmage. The quarterback will see how the defense is lined up and make a change to the play to take advantage of a weakness in the defense.

8. Screen Passes: A screen pass is designed to have the quarterback throw the ball to a running back who has blockers in front of him. This play is designed to catch the defense off guard and create a big gain.

9. Play-Action Fakes: A play-action fake is designed to deceive the defense by faking a handoff to a running back. This can create an opening for the quarterback to throw the ball downfield.

American football is a complex and dynamic sport that requires a diverse range of skills and abilities. A well-designed offensive strategy is essential for success in American football. By understanding the different formations, plays, and tactics used in American football, players and fans can better appreciate the strategy and excitement of this popular sport.

Running game

in American Football

In American football, the running game is an essential aspect of the offense. Running plays are designed to hand the ball off to a running back and have him run up the field, gaining yards and moving the ball closer to the end zone. Below we will we will explore the running game in American football, including the different types of running plays, the roles of the offensive players, and the strategies used to gain yardage on the ground.

Types of Running Plays

There are many different types of running plays used in American football, each designed to gain yards and move the ball up the field. Some of the most common types of running plays include:

1. Power Run: A power run is designed to have the offensive line block the defense and create a hole for the running back to run through. The running back will take the ball and run straight up the middle of the field, using his power and strength to gain yards.

2. Counter Run: A counter run is designed to fake a run in one direction and then have the running back run in the opposite direction. The offensive line will block in the opposite direction, creating confusion for the defense and allowing the running back to gain yards.

3. Sweep Run: A sweep run is designed to have the running back run around the outside of the offensive line. The offensive line will block in the direction of the run, creating a path for the running back to follow.

Roles of Offensive Players

The running game requires the cooperation and coordination of all of the offensive players. Each player has a specific role to play in the running game, and understanding these roles is essential for success on the ground. Some of the most important roles in the running game include:

4. Offensive Line: The offensive line is responsible for blocking the defense and creating holes for the running back to run through. The offensive line must work together and communicate to create successful running plays.

5. Running Back: The running back is responsible for running with the ball and gaining yards. The running back must have good vision, agility, and strength to be successful on the ground.

6. Quarterback: The quarterback is responsible for handing the ball off to the running back and calling plays at the line of scrimmage. The quarterback must have good communication skills and decision-making abilities to be successful in the running game.

Strategies

In addition to the specific types of running plays and the roles of the offensive players, there are also different strategies that can be used to gain yards on the ground. Some of the most common strategies used in the running game include:

7. Ball Security: Ball security is essential in the running game. The running back must hold onto the ball tightly and protect it from the defense. Fumbling the ball can result in a turnover and a lost opportunity to score.

8. Running Clock: Running the ball can be used to run down the clock and preserve a lead. By running the ball and keeping the clock moving, the offense can limit the number of possessions the opposing team has and reduce their chances of scoring.

9. Play-Action Pass: Running the ball can set up a play-action pass, where the quarterback fakes a run and then throws the ball downfield. This can catch the defense off guard and result in a big gain.

The running game is an essential aspect of the offense in American football. By understanding the different types of running plays, the roles of the offensive players, and the strategies used to gain yardage on the ground, players and fans can better appreciate the importance of the running game in this popular sport.

Passing game

in American Football

The passing game is an essential aspect of the offense in American football. Passing plays are designed to have the quarterback throw the ball downfield to a receiver, with the aim of gaining yards and scoring points. Below we will we will explore the passing game in American football, including the different types of passing plays, the roles of the offensive players, and the strategies used to gain yardage through the air.

Types of Passing Plays

There are many different types of passing plays used in American football, each designed to gain yards and move the ball up the field. Some of the most common types of passing plays include:

1. Screen Pass: A screen pass is designed to have the quarterback throw the ball to a receiver who is behind the line of scrimmage. The offensive linemen will block the defense, creating space for the receiver to run up the field.

2. Slant Route: A slant route is designed to have the receiver run at an angle across the field, catching the ball and running up the field. This play is designed to take advantage of holes in the defense.

3. Go Route: A go route is designed to have the receiver run straight down the field, catching the ball deep and gaining a lot of yards. This play is designed for speed receivers who can run past the defense.

Roles of Offensive Players

The passing game requires the cooperation and coordination of all of the offensive players. Each player has a specific role to play in the passing game, and understanding these roles is essential for success through the air. Some of the most important roles in the passing game include:

4. Offensive Line: The offensive line is responsible for protecting the quarterback from the defense. The offensive line must block the defense and give the quarterback time to throw the ball.

5. Quarterback: The quarterback is responsible for throwing the ball downfield and calling plays at the line of scrimmage. The quarterback must have good accuracy and decision-making abilities to be successful in the passing game.

6. Wide Receiver: The wide receiver is responsible for catching the ball and gaining yards. The wide receiver must have good hands, speed, and route-running abilities to be successful through the air.

Strategies

In addition to the specific types of passing plays and the roles of the offensive players, there are also different strategies that can be used to gain yards through the air. Some of the most common strategies used in the passing game include:

7. Play-Action Pass: A play-action pass is designed to fake a running play and then have the quarterback throw the ball downfield. This can catch the defense off guard and create an opening for the receiver.

8. Vertical Stretch: A vertical stretch is designed to have multiple receivers run deep routes, stretching the defense vertically and creating holes for other receivers to catch the ball underneath.

9. Run-Pass Option: A run-pass option is designed to have the quarterback read the defense and decide whether to hand the ball off or throw the ball downfield. This can create confusion for the defense and open up opportunities for big gains.

The passing game is an essential aspect of the offense in American football. By understanding the different types of passing plays, the roles of the offensive players, and the strategies used to gain yardage through the air, players and fans can better appreciate the importance of the passing game in this popular sport.

Play-action and trick plays

In American football, play-action and trick plays are often used to deceive the defense and create opportunities for big gains. These types of plays are designed to fake one type of play and then execute another, catching the defense off guard and creating openings for receivers or running backs. Below we will we will explore play-action and trick plays in American football, including their different types, how they work, and their role in offensive strategies.

Play-Action Plays

Play-action plays are designed to fake a running play and then have the quarterback throw the ball downfield. These types of plays can be effective in catching the defense off guard and creating openings for receivers to catch the ball. Play-action plays work by having the quarterback fake a handoff to the running back, causing the defense to focus on the running back and create openings in the secondary. The quarterback then throws the ball downfield to a receiver who is open.

There are several types of play-action plays used in American football, including the bootleg, waggle, and play-action pass. The bootleg is a play where the quarterback fakes a handoff to the running back and then runs in the opposite direction of the fake, usually with the option to throw the ball downfield. The waggle is a similar play where the quarterback fakes a handoff to the running back and then rolls out in the same direction as the fake, with the option to throw the ball downfield. The play-action pass is a more traditional play where the quarterback fakes a handoff to the running back and then drops back to pass.

Trick Plays

Trick plays are designed to deceive the defense and create opportunities for big gains. These types of plays can be risky, as they often involve unconventional methods or unexpected players, but they can also be very effective when executed correctly. Trick plays work by using unexpected methods or players to create confusion in the defense, opening up opportunities for receivers or running backs to gain yards.

There are several types of trick plays used in American football, including the flea flicker, reverse, and fake field goal or punt. The flea flicker is a play where the quarterback hands the ball off to a running back, who then pitches it back to the quarterback, who throws the ball downfield. The reverse is a play where the ball carrier hands the ball off to a teammate running in the opposite direction, creating confusion in the defense. The fake field goal or punt is a play where the kicking team lines up to kick the ball, but instead executes a trick play, such as a pass or a run.

Role in Offensive Strategies

Play-action and trick plays are important parts of offensive strategies in American football. They can be used to create openings in the defense and gain big yards. However, these types of plays can also be risky, as they rely on deception and can be difficult to execute. As a result, they are often used sparingly and strategically, as part of a larger offensive game plan.

Play-action and trick plays can also be used to complement other offensive strategies, such as the running game or the passing game. By using different types of plays and strategies, offensive coaches can keep the defense off balance and create opportunities for their players to gain yards and score points.

Play-action and trick plays are important aspects of offensive strategies in American football. These types of plays can be effective in catching the defense off guard and creating opportunities for big gains. However, they can also be risky, as they rely on deception and can be difficult to execute. By understanding the different types of play-action and trick plays and their role in offensive strategies, players and fans can better appreciate the complexity and excitement of this popular sport.

Basic Defensive Strategies

In American football, the defensive strategies are just as important as the offensive strategies. The defensive team aims to prevent the offensive team from scoring points and gaining yards. Below we will we will explore some of the basic defensive strategies used in American football, including the different formations, types of coverage, and tactics used to stop the offense.

Formations

The defensive formation is the way that the defensive players line up before the snap of the ball. There are many different types of formations used in American football, but some of the most common include:

1. 4-3 Formation: The 4-3 Formation features four defensive linemen and three linebackers. This formation is designed to stop the run and put pressure on the quarterback.

2. 3-4 Formation: The 3-4 Formation features three defensive linemen and four linebackers. This formation is designed to confuse the offense and create pressure on the quarterback.

3. Nickel Formation: The Nickel Formation features five defensive backs instead of the traditional four. This formation is designed to stop the pass and cover the receivers.

Coverage

Once the formation is set, the defense will use coverage schemes to try and stop the offense. There are many different types of coverage used in American football, but some of the most common include:

4. Man-to-Man Coverage: Man-to-Man Coverage is when each defensive player is responsible for covering a specific offensive player. This coverage is effective for shutting down a specific receiver or tight end.

5. Zone Coverage: Zone Coverage is when each defensive player is responsible for covering a specific area of the field. This coverage is effective for stopping the pass and preventing big plays.

6. Press Coverage: Press Coverage is when the defensive back lines up close to the receiver and tries to disrupt their route. This coverage is effective for preventing short passes and disrupting the timing of the offense.

Tactics

In addition to formations and coverage, the defense can use different tactics to gain an advantage over the offense. Some of the most common defensive tactics used in American football include:

7. Blitzing: Blitzing is when the defense sends more players than the offense can block. This tactic is designed to create pressure on the quarterback and disrupt the timing of the offense.

8. Stunting: Stunting is when defensive linemen switch positions before the snap of the ball, confusing the offensive linemen and creating openings for the defense to make a play.

9. Zone Blitzing: Zone Blitzing is when the defense sends extra players to blitz the quarterback, but also drops a defensive lineman into pass coverage. This tactic is designed to confuse the offense and create opportunities for turnovers.

American football is a complex and dynamic sport that requires a diverse range of skills and abilities. A well-designed defensive strategy is essential for success in American football. By understanding the different formations, types of coverage, and tactics used in American football, players and fans can better appreciate the strategy and excitement of this popular sport.

Man-to-man defense

In American football, man-to-man defense is a defensive strategy where each defensive player is responsible for covering a specific offensive player. This strategy is often used to shut down a specific receiver or tight end and prevent them from catching the ball. Below we will we will explore man-to-man defense in American football, including how it works, its strengths and weaknesses, and its role in defensive strategies.

How it Works

Man-to-man defense works by assigning each defensive player a specific offensive player to cover. The defender will follow the offensive player around the field, attempting to prevent them from catching the ball. This strategy is often used against a team that has a dominant receiver or tight end that the defense wants to shut down.

Man-to-man defense is often combined with other defensive strategies, such as blitzing or stunting. These tactics can create pressure on the quarterback and disrupt the timing of the offense, making it more difficult for them to complete passes.

Strengths and Weaknesses

Man-to-man defense has several strengths that make it an effective strategy in American football. Some of these strengths include:

1. Shutting Down a Specific Player: Man-to-man defense is effective for shutting down a specific receiver or tight end. By assigning a defender to cover them, the defense can limit their ability to catch the ball and gain yards.

2. Creating Opportunities for Turnovers: Man-to-man defense can create opportunities for turnovers, such as interceptions or fumbles. By closely covering each offensive player, the defense can take advantage of any mistakes or miscommunications.

3. Disrupting the Timing of the Offense: Man-to-man defense, when combined with blitzing or stunting, can disrupt the timing of the offense and make it more difficult for them to complete passes.

However, man-to-man defense also has several weaknesses that can be exploited by the offense. Some of these weaknesses include:

4. Creating Mismatches: Man-to-man defense can create mismatches if the offense has a receiver or tight end that is significantly faster or stronger than the defender covering them.

5. Leaving Openings in the Secondary: Man-to-man defense can leave openings in the secondary if the defender covering a specific player gets beaten or out of position.

6. Tiring Out Defenders: Man-to-man defense can be physically demanding, and defenders can become tired or fatigued over the course of a game, making it more difficult to maintain coverage.

Role in Defensive Strategies

Man-to-man defense is an important part of defensive strategies in American football. It can be used to shut down a specific receiver or tight end and prevent them from catching the ball. However, man-to-man defense is often combined with other defensive strategies, such as zone coverage or blitzing, to create a more effective defensive game plan.

Man-to-man defense is also used strategically throughout a game. It may be used to start a game, to shut down a specific player or group of players, or to make a crucial defensive stand in a key situation.

Man-to-man defense is an important strategy in American football, allowing defenders to closely cover specific offensive players and shut down their ability to catch the ball. By understanding the strengths and weaknesses of man-to-man defense and its role in defensive strategies, players and fans can better appreciate the complexity and strategy of this popular sport.

Zone defense

In American football, zone defense is a defensive strategy where each defensive player is responsible for covering a specific area of the field, rather than a specific offensive player. This strategy is often used to prevent big plays and prevent the offense from gaining yards through the air. Below we will we will explore zone defense in American football, including how it works, its strengths and weaknesses, and its role in defensive strategies.

How it Works

Zone defense works by assigning each defensive player a specific area of the field to cover. The defenders will work together to cover the entire field, preventing the offense from completing passes and gaining yards. This strategy is often used to prevent big plays, as it makes it difficult for the offense to find openings in the defense.

Zone defense is often combined with other defensive strategies, such as blitzing or stunting. These tactics can create pressure on the quarterback and disrupt the timing of the offense, making it more difficult for them to complete passes.

Strengths and Weaknesses

Zone defense has several strengths that make it an effective strategy in American football. Some of these strengths include:

1. Preventing Big Plays: Zone defense is effective for preventing big plays, as the defenders are responsible for covering specific areas of the field and preventing the offense from finding openings.

2. Limiting Yards After the Catch: Zone defense is effective for limiting yards after the catch, as the defenders are in position to make a tackle as soon as the ball is caught.

3. Allowing for More Opportunities for Turnovers: Zone defense can create more opportunities for turnovers, such as interceptions, as the defenders are in position to make a play on the ball.

However, zone defense also has several weaknesses that can be exploited by the offense. Some of these weaknesses include:

4. Leaving Openings in the Defense: Zone defense can leave openings in the defense if the defenders are not in the right position or if they get beaten by the offense.

5. Allowing for Short Gains: Zone defense can allow for short gains by the offense, as the defenders are not closely covering specific offensive players.

6. Making it More Difficult to Stop the Run: Zone defense can make it more difficult to stop the run, as the defenders are focused on stopping the pass.

Role in Defensive Strategies

Zone defense is an important part of defensive strategies in American football. It can be used to prevent big plays and limit yards after the catch. However, zone defense is often combined with other defensive strategies, such as man-to-man coverage or blitzing, to create a more effective defensive game plan.

Zone defense is also used strategically throughout a game. It may be used to prevent the offense from gaining yards through the air, to protect a lead, or to make a crucial defensive stand in a key situation.

Zone defense is an important strategy in American football, allowing defenders to cover specific areas of the field and prevent the offense from completing passes and gaining yards. By understanding the strengths and weaknesses of zone defense and its role in defensive strategies, players and fans can better appreciate the complexity and strategy of this popular sport.

Blitzing and pass rush

In American football, blitzing and pass rush are defensive strategies designed to put pressure on the quarterback and disrupt the timing of the offense. These strategies involve sending extra players, such as linebackers or defensive backs, to rush the quarterback and create opportunities for sacks or turnovers. Below we will we will explore blitzing and pass rush in American football, including how they work, their strengths and weaknesses, and their role in defensive strategies.

Blitzing

Blitzing is a defensive strategy where the defense sends more players than the offense can block, usually involving linebackers or defensive backs. The goal of blitzing is to create pressure on the quarterback and disrupt the timing of the offense. Blitzing can be a risky strategy, as it can leave the defense vulnerable to big plays if the quarterback is able to get the ball off quickly.

There are several types of blitzing strategies used in American football, including:

1. A-gap blitz: A-gap blitz is when the linebacker or defensive back rushes through the gap between the center and the guard. This is a popular blitzing strategy, as it can create pressure on the quarterback quickly.

2. B-gap blitz: B-gap blitz is when the linebacker or defensive back rushes through the gap between the guard and the tackle. This is a more risky blitzing strategy, as it can leave the defense vulnerable to the run.

3. Corner blitz: Corner blitz is when a cornerback rushes from the edge of the line of scrimmage. This is a less common blitzing strategy, as it leaves the defense vulnerable to deep passes.

Pass Rush

Pass rush is a defensive strategy that involves rushing the quarterback with the defensive line, usually involving defensive ends and defensive tackles. The goal of pass rush is to create pressure on the quarterback and disrupt the timing of the offense. Pass rush is a less risky strategy than blitzing, as it leaves more defenders in coverage to stop the pass.

There are several types of pass rushing strategies used in American football, including:

4. Bull rush: Bull rush is when the defensive lineman uses their strength to push the offensive lineman back and create pressure on the quarterback.

5. Swim move: Swim move is when the defensive lineman uses a quick motion to move past the offensive lineman and create pressure on the quarterback.

6. Spin move: Spin move is when the defensive lineman uses a spinning motion to move past the offensive lineman and create pressure on the quarterback.

Strengths and Weaknesses

Blitzing and pass rush have several strengths that make them effective strategies in American football. Some of these strengths include:

7. Creating Pressure on the Quarterback: Blitzing and pass rush are both effective for creating pressure on the quarterback and disrupting the timing of the offense.

8. Creating Opportunities for Sacks and Turnovers: Blitzing and pass rush can create opportunities for sacks and turnovers, as the defense can take advantage of any mistakes or miscommunications.

9. Forcing the Offense to Adjust: Blitzing and pass rush can force the offense to adjust their game plan and create openings in the defense.

However, blitzing and pass rush also have several weaknesses that can be exploited by the offense. Some of these weaknesses include:

10. Leaving Openings in the Defense: Blitzing and pass rush can leave openings in the defense if the defense is not able to get to the quarterback in time.

11. Leaving the Defense Vulnerable to Big Plays: Blitzing can leave the defense vulnerable to big plays if the quarterback is able to get the ball off quickly and find an open receiver.

12. Fatiguing Defenders: Blitzing and pass rush can be physically demanding, and defenders can become tired or fatigued over the course of a game, making it more difficult to maintain pressure on the quarterback.

The Quarterback

In American football, the quarterback is a key position on the offensive team. The quarterback is responsible for leading the offense, calling plays, and making decisions on the field. Below we will we will explore the role of the quarterback in American football, including their responsibilities, skills, and importance to the team.

Responsibilities

The quarterback is responsible for leading the offensive team and calling plays. They are the primary passer on the team, and are responsible for throwing the ball to receivers and running backs. The quarterback also has the ability to run the ball themselves, either as a designed play or as a scramble.

The quarterback's main responsibility is to move the ball down the field and score points. They must read the defense and make quick decisions about where to throw the ball or whether to run it themselves. The quarterback must also be aware of the clock, as time management is crucial in the game of football.

Skills

To be a successful quarterback in American football, there are several key skills that are necessary. Some of these skills include:

1. Arm Strength: The quarterback must be able to throw the ball accurately and with power, in order to make plays down the field.

2. Accuracy: The quarterback must be able to throw the ball accurately to receivers, and be able to place the ball in tight spots.

3. Decision Making: The quarterback must be able to read the defense and make quick decisions about where to throw the ball or whether to run it themselves.

4. Mobility: The quarterback must have the ability to move around in the pocket and avoid sacks, as well as the ability to scramble and run the ball themselves.

Importance to the Team

The quarterback is arguably the most important player on the offensive team, and their performance can make or break a game. A good quarterback can elevate the entire team and lead them to victory, while a poor quarterback can make it difficult for the team to score points and win games.

The quarterback also serves as a leader on the team, both on and off the field. They must be able to communicate effectively with their teammates, and inspire them to perform at their best. The quarterback must also be able to handle pressure and maintain composure, even in the most challenging situations.

The quarterback is a key position in American football, responsible for leading the offensive team and making crucial decisions on the field. They must possess a range of skills, including arm strength, accuracy, decision making, and mobility. The quarterback's performance is crucial to the success of the team, and their ability to inspire and lead their teammates is just as important as their physical abilities. By understanding the role of the quarterback in American football, players and fans can better appreciate the complexity and strategy of this popular sport.

Role and responsibilities

In American football, each player on the field has a specific role and set of responsibilities. These roles and responsibilities are crucial to the success of the team, as each player must work together to move the ball down the field and score points. Below we will we will explore the different roles and responsibilities of players in American football, including their positions and specific tasks.

Offensive Positions and Responsibilities

The offensive team in American football has several positions, each with its own set of responsibilities. These positions include:

1. Quarterback: The quarterback is responsible for leading the offense and calling plays. They are the primary passer on the team, and are responsible for throwing the ball to receivers and running backs. The quarterback must read the defense and make quick decisions about where to throw the ball or whether to run it themselves.

2. Running Back: The running back is responsible for carrying the ball and gaining yards on the ground. They must be able to run through tackles and find openings in the defense.

3. Wide Receiver: The wide receiver is responsible for catching the ball from the quarterback and gaining yards through the air. They must be able to run precise routes and make catches in traffic.

4. Tight End: The tight end is a versatile position, responsible for both catching the ball and blocking for the running back. They must be able to run routes and catch the ball, as well as block defenders in the running game.

5. Offensive Lineman: The offensive lineman is responsible for blocking defenders and protecting the quarterback. They must work together as a unit to create openings for the running back and provide time for the quarterback to throw the ball.

Defensive Positions and Responsibilities

The defensive team in American football also has several positions, each with its own set of responsibilities. These positions include:

6. Defensive Lineman: The defensive lineman is responsible for stopping the run and rushing the quarterback. They must be able to push back offensive linemen and get to the quarterback quickly.

7. Linebacker: The linebacker is responsible for stopping the run and covering receivers in the passing game. They must be able to read the offense and make quick decisions about where to go on the field.

8. Defensive Back: The defensive back is responsible for covering receivers and preventing big plays. They must be able to read the offense and react quickly to the ball.

Special Teams Positions and Responsibilities

Special teams in American football includes players who are responsible for kicking, punting, and returning the ball. These positions include:

9. Kicker: The kicker is responsible for kicking field goals and extra points. They must be accurate and able to kick the ball long distances.

10. Punter: The punter is responsible for punting the ball down the field, often when the offense is unable to score. They must be able to kick the ball high and far, and pin the opposing team deep in their own territory.

11. Kick Returner: The kick returner is responsible for catching the ball after a kickoff and returning it as far as possible. They must be able to run through tackles and find openings in the defense.

Each player in American football has a specific role and set of responsibilities, which are crucial to the success of the team. By understanding the positions and tasks of each player on the field, players and fans can better appreciate the complexity and strategy of this popular sport.

Styles of play

In American football, there are several different styles of play that teams can use to achieve success on the field. Each style of play has its own strengths and weaknesses, and the best teams are able to adapt and use a variety of styles to suit their opponents and the situation. Below we will we will explore some of the different styles of play in American football, including their characteristics and strategies.

Power Running

Power running is a style of play that involves running the ball repeatedly and relying on the offensive line to create openings in the defense. This style of play is often associated with teams that have big, physical running backs and strong offensive lines. The goal of power running is to wear down the defense and create opportunities for big gains on the ground.

To be successful with power running, teams must be able to dominate the line of scrimmage and create openings for the running back. The running back must be able to break tackles and run through defenders, and the offensive line must be able to block effectively. Power running can be effective in short-yardage situations and in grinding out the clock when trying to hold a lead.

Spread Offense

The spread offense is a style of play that involves spreading out the offensive players across the field and creating openings for quick passes and runs. This style of play is often associated with teams that have athletic quarterbacks and fast, agile receivers. The goal of the spread offense is to create mismatches and find openings in the defense.

To be successful with the spread offense, teams must be able to move the ball quickly and take advantage of openings in the defense. The quarterback must be able to read the defense and make quick decisions about where to throw the ball, and the receivers must be able to run precise routes and make catches in traffic. The spread offense can be effective in creating big plays and scoring quickly, but it can also leave the defense vulnerable to turnovers and big plays by the opposing team.

West Coast Offense

The West Coast offense is a style of play that involves short, precise passes and a high level of accuracy by the quarterback. This style of play is often associated with teams that have mobile quarterbacks and versatile receivers. The goal of the West Coast offense is to move the ball methodically down the field and create opportunities for touchdowns.

To be successful with the West Coast offense, teams must be able to make accurate passes and take advantage of openings in the defense. The quarterback must be able to read the defense and make quick decisions about where to throw the ball, and the receivers must be able to run precise routes and make catches in traffic. The West Coast offense can be effective in controlling the clock and keeping the opposing team's offense off the field, but it can also be vulnerable to turnovers and big plays by the opposing team.

Air Raid Offense

The Air Raid offense is a style of play that involves a high volume of passes and a focus on creating big plays through the air. This style of play is often associated with teams that have strong-armed quarterbacks and fast, athletic receivers. The goal of the Air Raid offense is to create opportunities for big gains through the air and put points on the board quickly.

To be successful with the Air Raid offense, teams must be able to throw the ball accurately and take advantage of openings in the defense. The quarterback must be able to read the defense and make quick decisions about where to throw the ball, and the receivers must be able to run precise routes and make catches in traffic. The Air Raid offense can be effective in creating big plays and putting points on the board quickly, but it can also be vulnerable to turnovers and big plays by the opposing team.

Great quarterbacks in history

The quarterback is the most important position in American football, responsible for leading the offense and making crucial decisions on the field. Over the years, there have been many great quarterbacks who have helped lead their teams to victory and become legends in the sport. Below we will we will explore some of the greatest quarterbacks in the history of American football, including their accomplishments and impact on the game.

Joe Montana

Joe Montana is widely regarded as one of the greatest quarterbacks of all time, and his record speaks for itself. Montana won four Super Bowl championships with the San Francisco 49ers, and was named Super Bowl MVP three times. Montana was known for his calm demeanor and ability to lead his team in pressure situations, earning him the nickname "Joe Cool". Montana is also known for "The Catch", a game-winning touchdown pass to Dwight Clark in the 1981 NFC Championship Game, which is considered one of the greatest plays in NFL history.

Tom Brady

Tom Brady is one of the most successful quarterbacks in NFL history, having won seven Super Bowl championships with the New England Patriots and Tampa Bay Buccaneers. Brady is known for his work ethic and leadership skills, as well as his ability to perform at a high level in pressure situations. Brady holds several NFL records, including most career touchdown passes and most career playoff wins by a quarterback. His success and longevity in the league have earned him the nickname "The GOAT", or greatest of all time.

Johnny Unitas

Johnny Unitas is often regarded as one of the greatest quarterbacks in NFL history, and his impact on the game cannot be overstated. Unitas played 18 seasons in the NFL, mostly with the Baltimore Colts, and was known for his strong arm and ability to read defenses. Unitas led the Colts to three NFL championships, and was named the league's MVP three times. Unitas is also known for his performance in the 1958 NFL Championship Game, often called "The Greatest Game Ever Played", in which he led the Colts to a thrilling overtime victory over the New York Giants.

Brett Favre

Brett Favre is a former quarterback who played for the Green Bay Packers, New York Jets, and Minnesota Vikings over his 20-year career in the NFL. Favre was known for his toughness and ability to make big plays, often in unconventional ways. Favre won one Super Bowl championship with the Packers, and was named the league's MVP three times. Favre also holds several NFL records, including most career touchdown passes and most consecutive starts by a quarterback.

Peyton Manning

Peyton Manning is one of the most accomplished quarterbacks in NFL history, having won two Super Bowl championships with the Indianapolis Colts and Denver Broncos. Manning is known for his intelligence and ability to read defenses, as well as his work ethic and leadership skills. Manning holds several NFL records, including most career passing yards and most career touchdown passes. Manning was named the league's MVP five times, and is widely regarded as one of the greatest quarterbacks of all time.

The quarterback position in American football is one of the most important positions on the field, and the players who excel in this role can have a huge impact on the success of their team. The quarterbacks mentioned Below are just a few of the many great players who have made a lasting impact on the sport, and their accomplishments and legacies continue to inspire players and fans today.

The Offensive Line

In American football, the offensive line is a crucial part of the team's success, responsible for blocking defenders and protecting the quarterback. The offensive line is made up of five players, and their job is to work together as a unit to create openings for the running back and provide time for the quarterback to throw the ball. Below we will we will explore the importance of the offensive line and the key characteristics and responsibilities of its players.

Importance of the Offensive Line

The offensive line is the backbone of the offense in American football, providing protection for the quarterback and creating openings for the running back. Without a strong offensive line, the offense would struggle to move the ball down the field and score points. The offensive line is often overlooked by casual fans, but its importance cannot be overstated.

Characteristics of Offensive Linemen

Offensive linemen are typically large, powerful players with good footwork and agility. They must be able to block defenders and create openings for the running back, while also protecting the quarterback from oncoming defenders. Offensive linemen must also be able to work together as a unit, communicating effectively to ensure that each player knows his responsibilities and can execute them effectively.

Responsibilities of Offensive Linemen

The five positions on the offensive line include the center, two guards, and two tackles. Each position has specific responsibilities and tasks to perform.

1. Center: The center is responsible for snapping the ball to the quarterback and making blocking assignments. The center must be able to read the defense and make quick decisions about where to block.

2. Guards: The guards are responsible for blocking defenders and creating openings for the running back. They must be able to pull and block in open space, as well as block effectively at the line of scrimmage.

3. Tackles: The tackles are responsible for protecting the quarterback and blocking defenders on the edge. They must be able to handle speed rushers and have good footwork to stay in front of the defender.

The offensive line must work together to create openings for the running back and protect the quarterback. They must communicate effectively and be able to adjust to different defensive schemes and strategies. The offensive line must also be able to adapt to different game situations, such as short-yardage situations and two-minute drills.

The offensive line is a crucial part of the success of the offense in American football, responsible for blocking defenders and protecting the quarterback. The offensive line is made up of five players, each with specific responsibilities and tasks to perform. Offensive linemen must be large and powerful, with good footwork and agility. They must be able to work together as a unit, communicating effectively and adjusting to different defensive schemes and strategies. The offensive line is often overlooked by casual fans, but its importance cannot be overstated. Without a strong offensive line, the offense would struggle to move the ball down the field and score points.

Position breakdown and responsibilities

In American football, each player on the field has a specific position and set of responsibilities. Understanding the roles and responsibilities of each position is essential for both players and fans in order to appreciate the complexities of the game. Below we will we will break down the positions on the field and explore their respective responsibilities.

Offense

Quarterback

The quarterback is the leader of the offense, responsible for throwing the ball and directing the team down the field. The quarterback must have good vision, decision-making skills, and accuracy in order to be successful. The quarterback is also responsible for calling audibles at the line of scrimmage to adjust to the defense.

Running Back

The running back is responsible for carrying the ball and gaining yards on the ground. Running backs must have good speed and agility, as well as the ability to break tackles and run through defenders. Running backs must also be able to catch the ball out of the backfield and block for the quarterback in passing situations.

Wide Receiver

Wide receivers are responsible for catching the ball and gaining yards through the air. Wide receivers must have good speed and agility, as well as the ability to run precise routes and make catches in traffic. Wide receivers must also be able to block for the running back in running situations.

Tight End

The tight end is a versatile position, responsible for both blocking and catching passes. Tight ends must have good size and strength to block effectively, as well as good hands and route-running ability to catch passes.

Offensive Line

1. The offensive line is responsible for blocking defenders and creating openings for the running back and protecting the quarterback. The offensive line is made up of five players: the center, two guards, and two tackles. Each position has specific responsibilities and tasks to perform, as discussed in a previous chapter.

Defense

Defensive Line

The defensive line is responsible for stopping the run and putting pressure on the quarterback. The defensive line is made up of three to four players, depending on the formation. Defensive linemen must have good size and strength to hold their ground and shed blockers, as well as quickness and agility to rush the passer.

Linebacker

Linebackers are responsible for both stopping the run and covering receivers in passing situations. Linebackers must have good size and strength to take on blockers, as well as good speed and agility to cover receivers. Linebackers must also have good instincts and the ability to read and react to the offense.

Cornerback

Cornerbacks are responsible for covering receivers and preventing them from catching passes. Cornerbacks must have good speed and agility, as well as the ability to read and react to the offense. Cornerbacks must also be able to tackle effectively in the open field.

Safety

Safeties are responsible for preventing big plays and providing support in both the run and pass defense. Safeties must have good speed and agility, as well as good instincts and the ability to read and react to the offense. Safeties must also be able to tackle effectively in the open field.

Each position on the field in American football has specific responsibilities and tasks to perform. Understanding the roles and responsibilities of each position is essential for both players and fans to appreciate the complexities of the game. From the quarterback to the offensive line to the defensive line, each position plays a crucial role in the success of the team.

Techniques and skills

In American football, techniques and skills are essential for players to be successful on the field. Different positions require different techniques and skills, but there are some fundamental techniques and skills that all players must master. Below we will we will explore some of the most important techniques and skills in American football.

Blocking

Blocking is one of the most important techniques in American football, and it is required for many positions on the field. Blocking involves using your body to prevent a defender from getting to the ball carrier or quarterback. There are several types of blocks, including drive blocking, cut blocking, and pass blocking.

Tackling

Tackling is another essential technique in American football, and it is required for both defensive and offensive players. Tackling involves using your body to bring down the ball carrier. Proper tackling technique involves getting low, wrapping up the ball carrier, and driving through the tackle.

Passing

Passing is a key skill for quarterbacks and receivers in American football. A good pass must be accurate, with the right amount of velocity and trajectory to reach the receiver. Quarterbacks must also have good footwork and throwing mechanics in order to make consistent and accurate passes.

Catching

Catching is another essential skill for receivers in American football. A good catch involves using your hands to secure the ball and bring it into your body. Receivers must also be able to catch passes in traffic and make catches at difficult angles.

Route Running

Route running is a skill required for receivers in American football. Route running involves running precise routes and making cuts at the right time in order to create separation from the defender. Good route runners must be able to read the defense and adjust their routes accordingly.

Footwork

Footwork is important for many positions in American football, including quarterbacks, running backs, and linemen. Good footwork involves using proper steps and angles to create leverage and maintain balance. Footwork is also important for agility and quickness, allowing players to change direction quickly and evade defenders.

Ball Security

Ball security is an essential skill for ball carriers in American football, including running backs and receivers. Good ball security involves holding the ball tightly with both hands and protecting it from the defender. Ball carriers must also be able to switch the ball to their other hand quickly and effectively.

Techniques and skills are essential for success in American football. From blocking and tackling to passing and catching, each position on the field requires specific techniques and skills. Mastering these fundamentals is crucial for players to perform at a high level and contribute to the success of the team.

Importance of the O-line

In American football, the offensive line (O-line) is one of the most important units on the field. The O-line consists of five players who work together to protect the quarterback and create openings for the running back. Without a strong offensive line, the offense would struggle to move the ball down the field and score points. Below we will we will explore the importance of the O-line and how it contributes to the success of the team.

Protection of the Quarterback

One of the most important roles of the O-line is to protect the quarterback. The quarterback is the leader of the offense and is responsible for throwing the ball and directing the team down the field. In order for the quarterback to be successful, he needs time in the pocket to make his reads and find open receivers. The O-line is responsible for creating a clean pocket for the quarterback, allowing him to set his feet and make accurate throws. The O-line must also be able to recognize and adjust to different defensive schemes and blitzes in order to protect the quarterback.

Opening Up Running Lanes

In addition to protecting the quarterback, the O-line is responsible for opening up running lanes for the running back. The running back is responsible for carrying the ball and gaining yards on the ground. The O-line must create openings by blocking defenders and creating gaps for the running back to run through. The O-line must also be able to adjust to different defensive schemes and adjust their blocking assignments accordingly.

Team Chemistry

The O-line is a unit that requires a great deal of communication and coordination in order to be successful. The O-line must work together as a cohesive unit, communicating effectively and making split-second decisions. This requires a high level of trust and chemistry between the players on the O-line. The O-line must be able to recognize each other's strengths and weaknesses and adjust their blocking assignments accordingly.

Leadership

The O-line is often considered the heart of the offense, and the players on the O-line are often the leaders of the team. The O-line must set the tone for the rest of the offense and provide a physical presence on the field. The O-line must also be able to make adjustments on the fly and make split-second decisions in order to be successful.

The O-line is one of the most important units on the field in American football. The O-line is responsible for protecting the quarterback and creating openings for the running back. The O-line must work together as a unit, communicating effectively and making split-second decisions. The O-line is often considered the heart of the offense, and the players on the O-line are often the leaders of the team. Without a strong offensive line, the offense would struggle to move the ball down the field and score points.

The Defensive Line

In American football, the defensive line is a crucial component of the defense. The defensive line is responsible for stopping the run and putting pressure on the quarterback. The defensive line is made up of three to four players, depending on the formation. Below we will we will explore the importance of the defensive line and the key characteristics and responsibilities of its players.

Importance of the Defensive Line

The defensive line is essential for the success of the defense in American football. The defensive line is responsible for stopping the run and putting pressure on the quarterback. Without a strong defensive line, the defense would struggle to control the line of scrimmage and stop the run. A strong defensive line can disrupt the timing of the offense and force the quarterback to make quick decisions, leading to turnovers and sacks.

Characteristics of Defensive Linemen

Defensive linemen must be large and strong to hold their ground and shed blockers. They must also be quick and agile to rush the passer and pursue the ball carrier. Defensive linemen must have good hand technique and footwork to effectively use their strength and leverage to overpower blockers. They must also have good instincts and the ability to read and react to the offense.

Responsibilities of Defensive Linemen

The three positions on the defensive line include the defensive tackle and defensive end. Each position has specific responsibilities and tasks to perform.

1. Defensive Tackle: The defensive tackle is responsible for stopping the run and pushing the pocket in the pass rush. The defensive tackle must be able to hold his ground against double teams and shed blocks in order to make tackles.

2. Defensive End: The defensive end is responsible for setting the edge and rushing the passer. The defensive end must be able to get around the offensive tackle and put pressure on the quarterback. The defensive end must also be able to hold his ground against the run and force the ball carrier back inside.

The defensive line must work together to control the line of scrimmage and disrupt the offense. They must communicate effectively and be able to adjust to different offensive schemes and strategies. The defensive line must also be able to adapt to different game situations, such as short-yardage situations and two-minute drills.

The defensive line is a crucial part of the defense in American football, responsible for stopping the run and putting pressure on the quarterback. The defensive line is made up of three to four players, each with specific responsibilities and tasks to perform. Defensive linemen must be large and strong, with good hand technique and footwork, as well as good instincts and the ability to read and react to the offense. The defensive line must work together as a unit, communicating effectively and adjusting to different offensive schemes and strategies. A strong defensive line can disrupt the timing of the offense and force turnovers and sacks.

Pass rushing and run stopping

In American football, the defensive line is responsible for both stopping the run and putting pressure on the quarterback. In order to be successful, defensive linemen must be able to effectively rush the passer and stop the run. Below we will we will explore the techniques and strategies used by defensive linemen to pass rush and stop the run.

Pass Rushing

Pass rushing is the act of pressuring the quarterback to make a quick decision, leading to sacks, turnovers, and incompletions. In order to effectively pass rush, defensive linemen must be quick and agile, with good hand technique and footwork. The defensive line must also work together to create pressure, with different players occupying blockers and creating openings for other players to get through.

One of the most effective pass-rushing techniques is the bull rush. The bull rush involves pushing the offensive lineman back with brute force and overpowering the blocker. Another effective technique is the swim move, which involves using quick hand movement to get around the blocker and get to the quarterback. Defensive linemen must also be able to use spin moves and club moves to create openings and get to the quarterback.

Stopping the Run

Stopping the run is another important responsibility of the defensive line. Stopping the run involves holding the line of scrimmage and preventing the ball carrier from gaining yardage. In order to stop the run, defensive linemen must be strong and powerful, with good leverage and hand technique. Defensive linemen must also be able to shed blockers and make tackles.

One effective technique for stopping the run is the two-gap technique. The two-gap technique involves holding the line of scrimmage and being responsible for two gaps on either side of the offensive lineman. This requires good strength and leverage, as well as the ability to read and react to the offense. Another effective technique is the one-gap technique, which involves attacking one gap and penetrating the offensive line to disrupt the play.

Strategies for Pass Rushing and Run Stopping

The defensive line must be able to adapt to different offensive schemes and strategies in order to be successful. In passing situations, the defensive line must be able to recognize and adjust to different offensive formations and blocking schemes. The defensive line must also be able to communicate effectively and make split-second decisions in order to create pressure on the quarterback.

In running situations, the defensive line must be able to hold their ground and maintain their gaps. The defensive line must also be able to recognize and adjust to different running plays, such as sweeps and traps. The defensive line must also be able to pursue the ball carrier and make tackles in the open field.

Pass rushing and run stopping are two essential responsibilities of the defensive line in American football. Effective pass rushing requires good hand technique, footwork, and teamwork, while effective run stopping requires strength, leverage, and the ability to shed blockers. The defensive line must be able to adapt to different offensive schemes and strategies and communicate effectively in order to be successful. With effective pass rushing and run stopping, the defensive line can disrupt the timing of the offense and prevent the opposing team from gaining yardage and scoring points.

Impact players

In American football, impact players are those who make a significant contribution to the success of their team. Impact players are often game-changers, capable of making big plays that swing the momentum of the game. Below we will we will explore the characteristics of impact players and the importance of their contributions to their team.

Characteristics of Impact Players

1. Talent: Impact players possess a high level of talent and skill, often possessing physical abilities that set them apart from other players. They may possess exceptional speed, strength, agility, or other physical attributes that make them difficult to stop or defend.

2. Consistency: Impact players are consistent performers, delivering strong performances week in and week out. They are reliable and often deliver their best performances in the biggest moments of the game.

3. Leadership: Impact players often serve as leaders on their team, inspiring their teammates and setting an example of hard work and dedication. They are often vocal in the locker room and on the field, helping to motivate their teammates and keep them focused on the task at hand.

4. Competitive Drive: Impact players possess a fierce competitive drive and a desire to win. They are often motivated by the challenge of facing tough opponents and relish the opportunity to make big plays in critical moments.

Importance of Impact Players

5. Momentum: Impact players have the ability to swing the momentum of the game with their big plays. A touchdown or interception can energize a team and shift the momentum in their favor, giving them a psychological edge over their opponents.

6. Confidence: Impact players instill confidence in their teammates, who are often inspired by their performance and leadership. When an impact player makes a big play, it sends a message to the rest of the team that anything is possible and that they can win the game.

7. Strategy: Impact players often force opposing teams to adjust their game plan in order to account for their presence. This can open up opportunities for other players to make big plays and contribute to the team's success.

8. Game Management: Impact players often dictate the pace and direction of the game, forcing opposing teams to adjust their strategy and play style. They often force opponents to make mistakes and capitalize on those mistakes to win the game.

Examples of Impact Players

9. Tom Brady: Tom Brady is widely considered one of the greatest impact players in NFL history. He has led his team to numerous Super Bowl victories and has a reputation for delivering clutch performances in critical moments.

10. J.J. Watt: J.J. Watt is a dominant defensive lineman who has been a force on the field for years. He has won multiple Defensive Player of the Year awards and is known for his ability to disrupt opposing offenses and make game-changing plays.

11. Odell Beckham Jr.: Odell Beckham Jr. is a dynamic wide receiver who has made numerous highlight-reel catches throughout his career. He has a reputation for making big plays in critical moments and is known for his ability to turn a short pass into a long touchdown.

12. Aaron Donald: Aaron Donald is one of the most dominant defensive players in the NFL. He is a three-time Defensive Player of the Year award winner and is known for his ability to disrupt opposing offenses and make game-changing plays.

Impact players are essential to the success of a football team. They possess exceptional talent and skill, as well as a fierce competitive drive and a desire to win. They inspire their teammates and often dictate the pace and direction of the game. With their ability to make big plays and shift the momentum of the game, impact players can be the difference between winning and losing.

Linebackers and Secondary

In American football, the linebackers and secondary are key components of the defense. The linebackers are responsible for stopping the run and covering receivers, while the secondary is responsible for covering receivers and making interceptions. Below we will we will explore the characteristics and responsibilities of the linebackers and secondary and their importance to the defense.

Linebackers

The linebackers are typically the most versatile players on the defense, responsible for stopping the run and covering receivers. The linebackers are usually positioned behind the defensive line and in front of the secondary. There are generally three to four linebackers on the field, depending on the defensive formation.

Characteristics of Linebackers

1. Athleticism: Linebackers must be strong, fast, and agile in order to stop the run and cover receivers. They must be able to tackle ball carriers and break up passes, as well as drop back into coverage and defend the pass.

2. Intelligence: Linebackers must have a high football IQ and the ability to read and react to the offense. They must be able to recognize offensive formations and make split-second decisions based on the offensive play.

3. Leadership: Linebackers are often leaders on the defense, responsible for making calls and adjustments based on the offensive formation. They must be able to communicate effectively with their teammates and help to motivate and inspire them.

Responsibilities of Linebackers

4. Stopping the Run: Linebackers are primarily responsible for stopping the run. They must be able to read and react to the offensive play and get to the ball carrier quickly in order to make a tackle.

5. Covering Receivers: Linebackers must also be able to drop back into coverage and cover receivers. They must be able to recognize when a receiver is running a route and stay with the receiver to prevent them from making a catch.

Secondary

The secondary is made up of the cornerbacks and safeties, responsible for covering receivers and making interceptions. The secondary is positioned behind the linebackers and is the last line of defense against the opposing offense.

Characteristics of the Secondary

6. Speed: The secondary must be fast and quick in order to keep up with the opposing receivers. They must be able to change direction quickly and stay with the receiver throughout the route.

7. Agility: The secondary must be agile in order to make quick cuts and adjustments to stay with the receiver. They must be able to react quickly to the ball and make interceptions.

8. Intelligence: The secondary must have a high football IQ and the ability to read and react to the offense. They must be able to recognize offensive formations and make split-second decisions based on the offensive play.

Responsibilities of the Secondary

9. Covering Receivers: The primary responsibility of the secondary is to cover the opposing receivers. They must be able to stay with the receiver throughout the route and prevent them from making a catch.

10. Making Interceptions: The secondary must also be able to make interceptions when the opportunity arises. They must be able to read the quarterback's eyes and jump in front of the receiver to make a play on the ball.

Importance of Linebackers and Secondary

The linebackers and secondary are crucial components of the defense in American football. They are responsible for stopping the run and covering receivers, as well as making interceptions and stopping big plays. With their athleticism, intelligence, and leadership, the linebackers and secondary can disrupt the timing of the offense and prevent the opposing team from scoring points.

In American football, the linebackers and secondary are essential components of the defense. The linebackers are responsible for stopping the run and covering receivers, while the secondary is responsible for covering receivers and making interceptions. With their athleticism, intelligence, and leadership, the linebackers and secondary can disrupt the timing of the offense

Coverage and tackling skills

In American football, coverage and tackling skills are essential for the defense to be successful. Coverage skills refer to the ability of defenders to cover receivers and prevent them from making catches, while tackling skills refer to the ability of defenders to make tackles and stop ball carriers. Below we will we will explore the techniques and strategies used by defenders to improve their coverage and tackling skills.

Coverage Skills

Coverage skills are essential for defenders to prevent the opposing team from completing passes and scoring touchdowns. Good coverage skills require speed, agility, and the ability to read the quarterback's eyes and react quickly to the ball. Defenders must also be able to anticipate the route of the receiver and stay with them throughout the play.

1. Press Coverage: In press coverage, the defender lines up directly in front of the receiver and attempts to disrupt their route. The defender uses physical contact to redirect the receiver and throw off their timing.

2. Zone Coverage: In zone coverage, the defender covers a specific area of the field rather than a specific receiver. The defender reads the quarterback's eyes and reacts to the ball, attempting to make a play on it.

3. Man-to-Man Coverage: In man-to-man coverage, the defender is responsible for covering a specific receiver. The defender stays with the receiver throughout the route, attempting to prevent them from making a catch.

Tackling Skills

Tackling skills are essential for defenders to stop the ball carrier and prevent them from gaining yards. Good tackling skills require strength, balance, and the ability to wrap up the ball carrier and bring them to the ground.

4. Form Tackling: In form tackling, the defender approaches the ball carrier with their head up and their eyes on the target. The defender wraps up the ball carrier with their arms and drives them to the ground using their legs.

5. Hit Tackling: In hit tackling, the defender approaches the ball carrier with force, using their shoulder or chest to hit the ball carrier and knock them to the ground.

6. Wrap Tackling: In wrap tackling, the defender wraps their arms around the ball carrier and brings them to the ground using their body weight.

Techniques to Improve Coverage and Tackling Skills

7. Footwork: Good footwork is essential for defenders to stay with the receiver and make tackles. Defenders must be able to quickly change direction and stay balanced while in coverage or pursuing the ball carrier.

8. Hand Placement: Hand placement is important for defenders to disrupt the route of the receiver and wrap up the ball carrier. Defenders must place their hands in the right position in order to maintain leverage and control.

9. Vision: Good vision is essential for defenders to anticipate the movements of the receiver and the ball carrier. Defenders must keep their eyes on the target and be aware of their surroundings in order to make the right decisions.

10. Strength and Conditioning: Good strength and conditioning are essential for defenders to maintain their speed and agility throughout the game. Defenders must be in top physical shape in order to keep up with the pace of the game and make tackles.

Coverage and tackling skills are essential for the defense to be successful in American football. Defenders must possess good footwork, hand placement, and vision in order to stay with the receiver and make tackles. With good strength and conditioning, defenders can maintain their speed and agility throughout the game and prevent the opposing team from scoring points. With good coverage and tackling skills, defenders can disrupt the timing of the offense and prevent the opposing team from gaining yards and scoring touchdowns.

Legendary players

American football has seen many legendary players throughout its history. These players have made significant contributions to the sport and have left a lasting impact on the game. Below we will we will explore some of the most legendary players in American football history and their impact on the sport.

Jim Brown

Jim Brown is widely regarded as one of the greatest players in NFL history. Brown played for the Cleveland Browns from 1957 to 1965 and was known for his incredible speed, power, and agility. He was a three-time NFL MVP and a nine-time Pro Bowl selection. Brown led the league in rushing yards in eight of his nine seasons and retired as the NFL's all-time leading rusher. He was inducted into the Pro Football Hall of Fame in 1971.

Walter Payton

Walter Payton, also known as "Sweetness," is another legendary player in NFL history. Payton played for the Chicago Bears from 1975 to 1987 and was known for his incredible speed and agility. He was a nine-time Pro Bowl selection and a two-time NFL MVP. Payton retired as the NFL's all-time leading rusher and was inducted into the Pro Football Hall of Fame in 1993. He was also known for his humanitarian work off the field, including his efforts to help children with cancer.

Joe Montana

Joe Montana is one of the greatest quarterbacks in NFL history. Montana played for the San Francisco 49ers from 1979 to 1992 and was known for his accuracy and clutch performances in big games. He won four Super Bowls with the 49ers and was named the Super Bowl MVP three times. Montana retired as the NFL's all-time leader in Super Bowl passing yards and was inducted into the Pro Football Hall of Fame in 2000.

Lawrence Taylor

Lawrence Taylor, also known as "LT," is one of the greatest defensive players in NFL history. Taylor played for the New York Giants from 1981 to 1993 and was known for his incredible speed and strength. He was a three-time NFL Defensive Player of the Year and was named the NFL MVP in 1986. Taylor helped lead the Giants to two Super Bowl victories and retired with 132.5 career sacks. He was inducted into the Pro Football Hall of Fame in 1999.

Jerry Rice

Jerry Rice is widely regarded as the greatest wide receiver in NFL history. Rice played for the San Francisco 49ers, Oakland Raiders, and Seattle Seahawks from 1985 to 2004 and was known for his incredible speed, hands, and route-running. He was a 13-time Pro Bowl selection and a three-time Super Bowl champion. Rice retired as the NFL's all-time leader in receptions, receiving yards, and touchdown catches. He was inducted into the Pro Football Hall of Fame in 2010.

The legendary players mentioned above are just a few examples of the many great players who have made significant contributions to the sport of American football. These players have set records, won championships, and inspired future generations of players. They have left a lasting impact on the game and have helped to make it the most popular sport in America.

The Running Backs

In American football, running backs are key players on the offense. Running backs are responsible for carrying the ball and gaining yards on the ground. They are also used in the passing game as receivers and blockers. Below we will we will explore the characteristics, responsibilities, and techniques used by running backs to be successful in American football.

Characteristics of Running Backs

1. Speed: Running backs must be fast and quick in order to break through the opposing defense and gain yards on the ground.

2. Agility: Running backs must be agile in order to make quick cuts and avoid tackles.

3. Power: Running backs must be strong and powerful in order to break through tackles and gain extra yards.

4. Vision: Running backs must have good vision in order to see openings in the opposing defense and make quick decisions.

Responsibilities of Running Backs

5. Carrying the Ball: The primary responsibility of a running back is to carry the ball and gain yards on the ground. Running backs must be able to read the offensive line and find the best running lanes.

6. Receiving the Ball: Running backs are also used in the passing game as receivers. They must be able to catch the ball and make plays in open space.

7. Blocking: Running backs are responsible for blocking on passing plays to protect the quarterback from the opposing defense.

Techniques to Improve Running Back Skills

8. Footwork: Good footwork is essential for running backs to make quick cuts and avoid tackles. Running backs must be able to change direction quickly and maintain balance while in motion.

9. Ball Security: Ball security is essential for running backs to prevent turnovers. Running backs must hold the ball high and tight to prevent it from being stripped by the opposing defense.

10. Vision: Good vision is essential for running backs to see openings in the opposing defense and make quick decisions. Running backs must be able to read the offensive line and find the best running lanes.

11. Tackling: Running backs must be able to break through tackles and gain extra yards. Running backs must use their power and quickness to break through tackles and gain extra yards.

Famous Running Backs in NFL History

Emmitt Smith

Emmitt Smith is one of the greatest running backs in NFL history. He played for the Dallas Cowboys from 1990 to 2002 and was known for his speed, agility, and power. He was a three-time Super Bowl champion and the NFL's all-time leading rusher with 18,355 yards. He was inducted into the Pro Football Hall of Fame in 2010.

Barry Sanders

Barry Sanders is another legendary running back in NFL history. He played for the Detroit Lions from 1989 to 1998 and was known for his incredible speed and agility. He won the NFL MVP award in 1997 and retired as the third all-time leading rusher with 15,269 yards. He was inducted into the Pro Football Hall of Fame in 2004.

Walter Payton

Walter Payton, also known as "Sweetness," was another legendary running back in NFL history. He played for the Chicago Bears from 1975 to 1987 and was known for his incredible speed and agility. He retired as the NFL's all-time leading rusher with 16,726 yards and was a nine-time Pro Bowl selection. He was inducted into the Pro Football Hall of Fame in 1993.

Running backs are key players on the offense in American football. They are responsible for carrying the ball and gaining yards on the ground, as well as blocking and receiving in the passing game. With their speed, agility, and power, running backs can make big plays and help lead their team to victory.

Types of running backs

In American football, there are different types of running backs that teams can utilize to fit their offensive scheme and game plan. Each type of running back brings a unique set of skills and strengths to the team. Below we will we will explore the different types of running backs in American football and their roles on the offense.

Power Backs

Power backs are running backs who rely on their strength and power to break through tackles and gain extra yards. Power backs are typically larger and heavier than other types of running backs and can push through the opposing defense to gain extra yards. They are often used in short-yardage situations, such as on third or fourth down, to gain the necessary yardage to keep the drive alive. Power backs can also be used to wear down the opposing defense throughout the game.

Speed Backs

Speed backs are running backs who rely on their speed and quickness to break through the opposing defense and gain yards on the ground. Speed backs are typically smaller and lighter than other types of running backs and can make quick cuts and changes of direction to avoid tackles. They are often used in outside running plays, such as sweeps and tosses, where they can use their speed to get to the edge of the field and gain extra yards. Speed backs can also be used in the passing game as receivers and are often used to create mismatches with slower defenders.

Dual-Threat Backs

Dual-threat backs are running backs who are equally skilled in running and receiving. These running backs can be used in a variety of ways, both on the ground and through the air, and can create mismatches for the opposing defense. Dual-threat backs are typically smaller and more agile than power backs, but can also be effective in short-yardage situations due to their versatility. They are often used in spread offenses, where they can create space and opportunities for the quarterback to make plays.

All-Purpose Backs

All-purpose backs are running backs who can contribute in a variety of ways on the offense. These running backs are typically versatile and can run, catch, and block effectively. All-purpose backs can be used in a variety of offensive schemes and can adapt to different situations and game plans. They are often used as a change of pace back, providing a different skill set and style of play to complement the starting running back.

Third-Down Backs

Third-down backs are running backs who are used primarily on third down situations, such as passing plays and blitz pickups. These running backs are typically smaller and quicker than other types of running backs and are used in passing situations to catch the ball out of the backfield or to pick up blitzing defenders. Third-down backs are also used in two-minute drills, where time is of the essence, and a quick and efficient offense is needed to move the ball down the field.

In conclusion, there are different types of running backs in American football that teams can utilize to fit their offensive scheme and game plan. Power backs rely on their strength and power to break through the opposing defense, while speed backs rely on their speed and quickness to make quick cuts and gain extra yards. Dual-threat backs are equally skilled in running and receiving, while all-purpose backs can contribute in a variety of ways on the offense. Third-down backs are used primarily on third down situations, such as passing plays and blitz pickups. Understanding the different types of running backs can help teams build a more effective and efficient offense.

Ball carrying and blocking

1. In American football, running backs have two primary responsibilities: carrying the ball and blocking. Ball carrying and blocking are essential skills for running backs to be successful on the offense. Below we will we will explore the techniques and strategies used by running backs for ball carrying and blocking.

Ball Carrying Techniques

2. High and Tight: One of the most important ball carrying techniques is holding the ball high and tight. Running backs must hold the ball with both hands, high and tight to their chest, to prevent the ball from being stripped by the opposing defense. Running backs must also use their forearm to protect the ball and maintain a strong grip.

3. Vision: Good vision is essential for running backs to see openings in the opposing defense and make quick decisions. Running backs must be able to read the offensive line and find the best running lanes. They must also be able to anticipate the movements of the opposing defense and make quick adjustments to their running path.

4. Footwork: Good footwork is essential for running backs to make quick cuts and avoid tackles. Running backs must be able to change direction quickly and maintain balance while in motion. They must also be able to accelerate quickly to get through openings in the defense.

5. Physicality: Running backs must be able to use their strength and power to break through tackles and gain extra yards. They must be able to absorb contact from the opposing defense and keep their legs moving to gain extra yards.

Blocking Techniques

6. Pass Blocking: Pass blocking is an important blocking technique for running backs. Running backs must be able to pick up blitzing defenders and protect the quarterback from being sacked. Running backs must be able to recognize the blitzing defender and use their body to block them from reaching the quarterback.

7. Run Blocking: Run blocking is another important blocking technique for running backs. Running backs must be able to use their body to create openings for the ball carrier. Running backs must be able to read the defensive line and make quick decisions about which defender to block.

8. Technique: Good blocking technique is essential for running backs to be successful in blocking. Running backs must be able to use their hands, feet, and body to create a strong blocking position. They must also be able to maintain balance and leverage while blocking.

9. Communication: Communication is essential for running backs to be successful in blocking. Running backs must be able to communicate with the offensive line and quarterback to understand the blocking assignments and adjust their position accordingly.

In conclusion, ball carrying and blocking are essential skills for running backs to be successful in American football. Ball carrying techniques such as high and tight ball security, good vision, quick footwork, and physicality are important for running backs to gain yards on the ground. Blocking techniques such as pass blocking, run blocking, good technique, and communication are important for running backs to protect the quarterback and create openings for the ball carrier. Understanding these techniques and strategies can help running backs to be more effective and efficient on the field.

Notable running backs in history

Running backs have been an integral part of American football for decades. Over the years, many great running backs have made their mark on the game, leaving their names and legacies in the record books. Below we will we will explore some of the most notable running backs in the history of American football.

Jim Brown

Jim Brown is widely regarded as one of the greatest running backs in the history of American football. He played for the Cleveland Browns from 1957 to 1965 and was known for his power and speed on the field. He retired as the NFL's all-time leading rusher with 12,312 yards and was a nine-time Pro Bowl selection. Brown was also a three-time NFL MVP and helped lead the Browns to a championship in 1964. He was inducted into the Pro Football Hall of Fame in 1971.

Walter Payton

Walter Payton, also known as "Sweetness," was another legendary running back in NFL history. He played for the Chicago Bears from 1975 to 1987 and was known for his incredible speed and agility. He retired as the NFL's all-time leading rusher with 16,726 yards and was a nine-time Pro Bowl selection. Payton was also a Super Bowl champion and won the NFL MVP award in 1977. He was inducted into the Pro Football Hall of Fame in 1993.

Barry Sanders

Barry Sanders is another legendary running back in NFL history. He played for the Detroit Lions from 1989 to 1998 and was known for his incredible speed and agility. He retired as the third all-time leading rusher with 15,269 yards and was a 10-time Pro Bowl selection. Sanders won the NFL MVP award in 1997 and was inducted into the Pro Football Hall of Fame in 2004.

Emmitt Smith

Emmitt Smith is one of the greatest running backs in NFL history. He played for the Dallas Cowboys from 1990 to 2002 and was known for his speed, agility, and power. He was a three-time Super Bowl champion and the NFL's all-time leading rusher with 18,355 yards. Smith was also a eight-time Pro Bowl selection and won the NFL MVP award in 1993. He was inducted into the Pro Football Hall of Fame in 2010.

Gale Sayers

Gale Sayers, also known as "The Kansas Comet," was another great running back in NFL history. He played for the Chicago Bears from 1965 to 1971 and was known for his speed and agility. Sayers was a five-time Pro Bowl selection and was named the NFL Rookie of the Year in 1965. He retired with 4,956 rushing yards and 39 touchdowns. Sayers was inducted into the Pro Football Hall of Fame in 1977.

O.J. Simpson

O.J. Simpson, also known as "The Juice," was a legendary running back in NFL history. He played for the Buffalo Bills and San Francisco 49ers from 1969 to 1979 and was known for his speed and agility. Simpson won the NFL rushing title four times and was a six-time Pro Bowl selection. He retired with 11,236 rushing yards and 61 touchdowns. Simpson was inducted into the Pro Football Hall of Fame in 1985.

The Wide Receivers

In American football, wide receivers are a crucial part of the offense. They are responsible for catching passes from the quarterback and gaining yards through the air. Below we will we will explore the position of wide receivers, their roles, techniques, and some of the greatest players to have played the position.

Wide Receivers' Roles

The primary role of a wide receiver is to catch passes from the quarterback and gain yards through the air. Wide receivers must be fast, agile, and able to change direction quickly to create separation from defenders. They must also have good hands and be able to make difficult catches under pressure.

In addition to catching passes, wide receivers are also responsible for running routes and creating openings for other receivers. They must be able to read the opposing defense and adjust their routes accordingly. Wide receivers also play a role in blocking, particularly on running plays. They must be able to use their body to block defenders and create openings for the ball carrier.

Wide Receivers' Techniques

1. Route Running: Route running is one of the most important techniques for wide receivers. They must be able to run precise routes and create separation from defenders. Good route running involves quick changes of direction and the ability to read the defense.

2. Hands: Wide receivers must have good hands and be able to make difficult catches. They must be able to catch the ball cleanly and securely, even when defenders are in close proximity.

3. Footwork: Good footwork is essential for wide receivers to create separation from defenders. They must be able to make quick cuts and changes of direction to create openings for themselves.

4. Body Control: Body control is another important technique for wide receivers. They must be able to control their body in mid-air and make acrobatic catches. They must also be able to maintain their balance after making a catch and avoid being tackled.

Greatest Wide Receivers in History

5. Jerry Rice: Jerry Rice is widely considered to be the greatest wide receiver in NFL history. He played for the San Francisco 49ers from 1985 to 2000 and was known for his incredible hands and route running. Rice retired as the NFL's all-time leading receiver with 22,895 yards and 197 touchdowns.

6. Randy Moss: Randy Moss was one of the most dominant wide receivers in NFL history. He played for several teams, including the Minnesota Vikings, New England Patriots, and San Francisco 49ers. Moss was known for his incredible speed and ability to make difficult catches. He retired with 15,292 receiving yards and 156 touchdowns.

7. Terrell Owens: Terrell Owens was another great wide receiver in NFL history. He played for several teams, including the San Francisco 49ers, Dallas Cowboys, and Philadelphia Eagles. Owens was known for his incredible athleticism and ability to make acrobatic catches. He retired with 15,934 receiving yards and 153 touchdowns.

8. Larry Fitzgerald: Larry Fitzgerald is one of the greatest wide receivers in NFL history. He has played for the Arizona Cardinals since 2004 and has been named to the Pro Bowl 11 times. Fitzgerald is known for his route running and ability to make clutch catches. He has amassed 17,492 receiving yards and 121 touchdowns in his career.

In conclusion, wide receivers are an essential part of the offense in American football. They are responsible for catching passes from the quarterback and gaining yards through the air. Wide receivers must be fast, agile, and able to change direction quickly to create separation from defenders. Jerry Rice, Randy Moss, Terrell Owens, and Larry Fitzgerald are just a few of the greatest wide receivers to have played the position. Their skills and techniques have helped shape the position and contributed to the success of their teams.

Types of wide receivers

In American football, wide receivers are an essential part of the offense, responsible for catching passes and gaining yards through the air. There are different types of wide receivers, each with their own set of skills and roles on the field. Below we will we will explore the different types of wide receivers, their roles, and some of the greatest players to have played each position.

Split End

The split end is usually the primary receiver on the offense. They line up on the line of scrimmage, furthest from the quarterback, and are responsible for running deep routes and stretching the field. Split ends must be fast and agile, with excellent route running skills and the ability to make difficult catches under pressure.

Some of the greatest split ends in NFL history include Don Hutson, Raymond Berry, and Lance Alworth. These players were known for their ability to make deep catches and stretch the field, creating openings for other receivers.

Flanker

The flanker is another type of wide receiver that lines up on the line of scrimmage, but closer to the quarterback than the split end. Flankers are responsible for running intermediate routes, such as slants and curls, and are often used to create openings for other receivers.

Some of the greatest flankers in NFL history include Jerry Rice, Art Monk, and Michael Irvin. These players were known for their ability to make quick catches and gain yards after the catch.

Slot Receiver

The slot receiver lines up off the line of scrimmage, between the offensive line and the split end or flanker. Slot receivers are responsible for running short to intermediate routes and are often used as a safety valve for the quarterback.

Some of the greatest slot receivers in NFL history include Wes Welker, Julian Edelman, and Hines Ward. These players were known for their ability to make quick, short catches and gain yards after the catch.

Tight End

While not technically a wide receiver, tight ends are often used as receivers in the offense. They line up on the line of scrimmage, next to the offensive tackles, and are responsible for running routes and catching passes. Tight ends are usually bigger and stronger than wide receivers, and are often used in the red zone and on third downs.

Some of the greatest tight ends in NFL history include Tony Gonzalez, Rob Gronkowski, and Shannon Sharpe. These players were known for their ability to make difficult catches and gain yards after the catch.

In conclusion, there are different types of wide receivers in American football, each with their own set of skills and roles on the field. Split ends are responsible for stretching the field and making deep catches, flankers are responsible for running intermediate routes, slot receivers are responsible for short to intermediate routes, and tight ends are usually bigger and stronger and are used in the red zone and on third downs. Some of the greatest wide receivers in NFL history have played each of these positions, contributing to the success of their teams and leaving their legacies on the field.

Route running and catching

In American football, wide receivers are responsible for catching passes from the quarterback and gaining yards through the air. Route running and catching are two of the most important skills for wide receivers. Below we will we will explore the techniques and strategies involved in route running and catching.

Route Running

Route running is the ability to run precise routes and create separation from defenders. Good route running involves quick changes of direction and the ability to read the defense. There are several techniques involved in route running:

1. Stance: The stance is the starting position before running a route. A good stance involves a wide base, knees bent, and weight balanced on the balls of the feet.

2. Footwork: Footwork is an essential part of route running. Wide receivers must be able to make quick cuts and changes of direction to create openings for themselves. They must also be able to use their feet to deceive the defender and create separation.

3. Timing: Timing is critical in route running. Wide receivers must be able to time their route so that they are in the right place at the right time to catch the ball. This involves reading the defense and adjusting their route accordingly.

4. Body Position: Body position is another important technique in route running. Wide receivers must be able to use their body to shield the ball from defenders and create separation. They must also be able to make adjustments to their body position to make difficult catches.

Catching

Catching is the ability to catch the ball cleanly and securely, even when defenders are in close proximity. There are several techniques involved in catching:

5. Hand Placement: Hand placement is crucial in catching. Wide receivers must be able to position their hands so that they can catch the ball cleanly and securely. They must also be able to adjust their hand position to make difficult catches.

6. Hand-Eye Coordination: Hand-eye coordination is another important skill in catching. Wide receivers must be able to track the ball with their eyes and position their hands to catch it.

7. Body Control: Body control is essential in making difficult catches. Wide receivers must be able to control their body in mid-air and make acrobatic catches. They must also be able to maintain their balance after making a catch and avoid being tackled.

8. Concentration: Concentration is critical in catching. Wide receivers must be able to maintain their focus and concentration even when defenders are in close proximity. They must also be able to block out distractions and focus on catching the ball.

Strategies for Route Running and Catching

9. Visualization: Visualization is a technique used by many wide receivers to improve their route running and catching skills. By visualizing themselves running routes and making catches, they can improve their timing, footwork, and hand placement.

10. Practice: Practice is essential in improving route running and catching skills. Wide receivers must spend time practicing their footwork, timing, and hand placement. They must also practice making difficult catches and maintaining their concentration in the face of distractions.

11. Film Study: Film study is another strategy used by wide receivers to improve their skills. By watching game film, they can identify weaknesses in their route running and catching, as well as identify patterns in the opposing defense.

In conclusion, route running and catching are two of the most important skills for wide receivers in American football. Good route running involves quick changes of direction, timing, and body position. Catching involves hand placement, hand-eye coordination, body control, and concentration. By using strategies such as visualization, practice, and film study, wide receivers can improve their skills and become more effective on the field.

All-time greats

American football has seen many great players throughout its history, each contributing to the sport's evolution and popularity. From quarterbacks to running backs, wide receivers to defensive players, there have been many legendary players who have left their mark on the game. Below we will we will explore some of the all-time greats of American football and their contributions to the sport.

Quarterbacks

Quarterbacks are often considered the most important position in American football, responsible for leading the offense and making decisions on the field. Some of the greatest quarterbacks in NFL history include:

1. Tom Brady: Tom Brady is widely considered to be one of the greatest quarterbacks in NFL history. He has won seven Super Bowl championships and has been named Super Bowl MVP five times. He has thrown for over 80,000 yards and has over 600 touchdown passes in his career.

2. Joe Montana: Joe Montana is another legendary quarterback who led the San Francisco 49ers to four Super Bowl championships in the 1980s. He was known for his clutch performances in big games, earning him the nickname "Joe Cool". He retired with over 40,000 passing yards and 273 touchdown passes.

3. Johnny Unitas: Johnny Unitas is considered by many to be the greatest quarterback of the pre-Super Bowl era. He played for the Baltimore Colts in the 1950s and 60s and helped lead the team to three NFL championships. He retired with over 40,000 passing yards and 290 touchdown passes.

Running Backs

Running backs are responsible for running with the ball and gaining yards on the ground. Some of the greatest running backs in NFL history include:

4. Jim Brown: Jim Brown is widely considered to be one of the greatest running backs in NFL history. He played for the Cleveland Browns in the 1950s and 60s and led the league in rushing eight times. He retired with over 12,000 rushing yards and 106 rushing touchdowns.

5. Walter Payton: Walter Payton, also known as "Sweetness", was one of the most dominant running backs in NFL history. He played for the Chicago Bears in the 1970s and 80s and retired with over 16,000 rushing yards and 110 rushing touchdowns.

6. Barry Sanders: Barry Sanders was known for his incredible speed and agility on the field. He played for the Detroit Lions in the 1990s and retired with over 15,000 rushing yards and 99 rushing touchdowns.

Wide Receivers

Wide receivers are responsible for catching passes and gaining yards through the air. Some of the greatest wide receivers in NFL history include:

7. Jerry Rice: Jerry Rice is widely considered to be the greatest wide receiver in NFL history. He played for the San Francisco 49ers in the 1980s and 90s and retired with over 22,000 receiving yards and 197 receiving touchdowns.

8. Randy Moss: Randy Moss was one of the most dominant wide receivers in NFL history. He played for several teams, including the Minnesota Vikings, New England Patriots, and San Francisco 49ers. Moss retired with over 15,000 receiving yards and 156 receiving touchdowns.

9. Calvin Johnson: Calvin Johnson, also known as "Megatron", was known for his incredible size and athleticism on the field. He played for the Detroit Lions in the 2000s and retired with over 11,000 receiving yards and 83 receiving touchdowns.

Defensive Players

Defensive players are responsible for stopping the opposing team's offense and preventing them from scoring points. Some of the greatest defensive players in NFL history include:

10. Lawrence Taylor: Lawrence Taylor, also known as "LT", was one of the most dominant defensive players in NFL history.

Kickers and punters

Kickers and punters may not get as much attention as other positions in American football, but their contributions are critical to the success of a team. Below we will we will explore the roles of kickers and punters, as well as some of the all-time greats in these positions.

Kickers

Kickers are responsible for kicking field goals and extra points after touchdowns. They also handle kickoffs, which begin each half and follow a score. A kicker's accuracy is critical in close games, where a single missed field goal can make the difference between a win and a loss.

One of the greatest kickers in NFL history is Adam Vinatieri. He played for several teams, including the New England Patriots and Indianapolis Colts, and holds the record for most career points scored by a kicker with over 2,600 points. He is also known for making several clutch kicks in key moments, including game-winning field goals in Super Bowls XXXVI and XXXVIII.

Another great kicker is Morten Andersen, who played for several teams over his career, including the New Orleans Saints and Atlanta Falcons. He holds the record for most career field goals made with 565 and is second all-time in career points scored with over 2,500 points.

Punters

Punters are responsible for kicking the ball downfield on fourth down when the offense cannot convert a first down. The goal of a punter is to kick the ball as far as possible while also trying to pin the opposing team deep in their own territory.

One of the greatest punters in NFL history is Ray Guy. He played for the Oakland Raiders in the 1970s and 80s and is known for his incredible leg strength and accuracy. He was the first punter ever selected in the first round of the NFL draft and was named to seven Pro Bowls over his career.

Another great punter is Shane Lechler, who played for several teams over his career, including the Houston Texans and Oakland Raiders. He holds the record for most career punting yards with over 68,000 yards and is a seven-time Pro Bowler.

Importance of Kickers and Punters

Kickers and punters may not get as much attention as other positions in American football, but their contributions are critical to the success of a team. A missed field goal or a poorly executed punt can change the momentum of a game and give the opposing team an advantage.

Kickers and punters also play a critical role in special teams, which includes kickoffs, punts, and field goal attempts. Special teams can have a significant impact on the outcome of a game, and kickers and punters are often called upon to make key plays in critical moments.

In conclusion, kickers and punters play a critical role in American football, even if they do not get as much attention as other positions. Their accuracy and leg strength can make a significant impact on the outcome of a game, and their contributions to special teams are essential for the success of a team. Some of the all-time greats in these positions, including Adam Vinatieri, Morten Andersen, Ray Guy, and Shane Lechler, have left their mark on the sport and continue to be remembered for their incredible skill and precision on the field.

Return specialists

Return specialists are players on special teams who are responsible for returning kickoffs and punts. These players have a unique skill set that includes speed, agility, and the ability to read the field and make quick decisions. Below we will we will explore the role of return specialists in American football and some of the greatest return specialists in NFL history.

The Role of Return Specialists

Return specialists play a critical role in American football, as they are responsible for setting up their team's offense with good field position. By returning kickoffs and punts, they can help their team gain valuable yardage and potentially score points.

In addition to setting up the offense, return specialists can also directly impact the outcome of a game by scoring touchdowns themselves. A well-executed return can swing the momentum of a game and give a team a significant advantage.

Return specialists must be able to navigate through traffic, read blocks, and make quick decisions on the field. They must also have excellent ball-handling skills to avoid fumbles, as turnovers can have a significant impact on the outcome of a game.

Greatest Return Specialists in NFL History

1. Devin Hester: Devin Hester is widely considered to be one of the greatest return specialists in NFL history. He played for several teams over his career, including the Chicago Bears and Atlanta Falcons, and holds the record for most career return touchdowns with 20. He was named to the Pro Bowl four times and was a first-team All-Pro three times.

2. Dante Hall: Dante Hall, also known as the "Human Joystick", was known for his incredible agility and quickness on the field. He played for several teams, including the Kansas City Chiefs and St. Louis Rams, and is second all-time in career return touchdowns with 12. He was named to the Pro Bowl three times and was a first-team All-Pro once.

3. Joshua Cribbs: Joshua Cribbs played for the Cleveland Browns and Oakland Raiders and is known for his versatility as both a return specialist and wide receiver. He holds the record for most career kickoff return yards with over 11,000 yards and has eight career return touchdowns. He was named to the Pro Bowl three times.

4. Gale Sayers: Gale Sayers is considered by many to be one of the greatest running backs in NFL history, but he was also an exceptional return specialist. He played for the Chicago Bears in the 1960s and holds the record for most touchdowns in a rookie season with 22. He was named to the Pro Bowl four times and was a first-team All-Pro five times.

5. Mel Gray: Mel Gray played for several teams, including the Detroit Lions and Arizona Cardinals, and is known for his speed and agility on the field. He holds the record for most career kickoff return touchdowns with six and was named to the Pro Bowl four times.

Importance of Return Specialists

Return specialists may not get as much attention as other positions in American football, but their contributions are critical to the success of a team. By setting up the offense with good field position or scoring touchdowns themselves, they can swing the momentum of a game and give their team a significant advantage.

Return specialists also play a critical role in special teams, which includes kickoffs, punts, and field goal attempts. Special teams can have a significant impact on the outcome of a game, and return specialists are often called upon to make key plays in critical moments.

In conclusion, return specialists play a critical role in American football, even if they do not get as much attention as other positions. Their speed, agility, and ability to read the field can make a significant impact on the outcome of a game, and their contributions to special teams are essential for the success of a team. Some of the all-time greats in

Long snappers and coverage units

Long snappers and coverage units are two important components of special teams in American football. Below we will we will explore the role of long snappers and coverage units and their importance in the game.

Long Snappers

Long snappers are responsible for snapping the ball to the punter or holder for field goal and extra point attempts. This may seem like a simple task, but it requires a high level of skill and precision. Long snappers must be able to accurately snap the ball over a distance of 15 yards or more, while also being aware of the defensive players rushing towards them.

Long snappers are often overlooked in the game of football, but their importance cannot be overstated. A poor snap can result in a blocked punt or a missed field goal, which can have a significant impact on the outcome of a game.

Coverage Units

Coverage units are made up of players who are responsible for preventing the opposing team's return specialist from gaining yardage or scoring a touchdown. This requires a high level of teamwork and coordination, as players must stay in their lanes and maintain their coverage assignments.

Coverage units are often led by the kicker or punter, who can help direct the players on the field. These units must be able to quickly react to the opposing team's return, while also being aware of any potential trick plays or fakeouts.

Importance of Long Snappers and Coverage Units

Long snappers and coverage units may not get as much attention as other positions in American football, but their contributions are critical to the success of a team. A poor snap or a breakdown in coverage can have a significant impact on the outcome of a game.

Long snappers and coverage units are also important because they are often called upon in critical moments of the game. For example, a team may need a field goal or a punt in the final minutes of a game, and a successful snap and coverage can help seal a victory.

All-Time Greats

Long snappers and coverage units are often overlooked in the game of football, but there have been several players who have excelled in these positions over the years.

One of the greatest long snappers in NFL history is Trey Junkin, who played for several teams over his career, including the New York Giants and Arizona Cardinals. He played in over 260 games and was known for his accuracy and consistency as a long snapper.

Another great long snapper is Patrick Mannelly, who played his entire career for the Chicago Bears. He played in over 250 games and was known for his durability and consistency, as well as his leadership on special teams.

In terms of coverage units, the 2000 Baltimore Ravens are often regarded as one of the best in NFL history. Led by kicker Matt Stover and punter Kyle Richardson, the Ravens had a dominant coverage unit that allowed only 4.6 yards per punt return and no touchdowns all season.

In conclusion, long snappers and coverage units are critical components of special teams in American football. Their contributions are often overlooked, but their importance cannot be overstated. A successful snap or a well-executed coverage can have a significant impact on the outcome of a game. Some of the all-time greats in these positions, such as Trey Junkin, Patrick Mannelly, and the 2000 Baltimore Ravens, have left their mark on the game and continue to be remembered for their contributions to special teams.

Coaching and Team Management

Coaching and team management are critical components of success in American football. Below we will we will explore the role of coaches and team managers, the qualities of effective coaches, and some of the greatest coaches in NFL history.

The Role of Coaches and Team Managers

Coaches and team managers are responsible for leading and managing a football team. They must develop strategies and game plans, coordinate practices and workouts, and make personnel decisions such as choosing which players to start or substitute during games.

Coaches and team managers must also be able to effectively communicate with their players and staff, providing feedback and guidance on performance and helping to build a positive team culture. They must be able to motivate their players and foster a sense of unity and teamwork, which can be critical to success on the field.

Qualities of Effective Coaches

Effective coaches possess several key qualities that enable them to lead and manage their team successfully. One of the most important qualities is strong communication skills. Coaches must be able to clearly convey their expectations to their players and staff, and provide constructive feedback in a way that is both effective and respectful.

Another important quality is leadership. Coaches must be able to inspire and motivate their players, and provide a clear vision for what the team is trying to achieve. They must also be able to make tough decisions and take responsibility for the outcomes of those decisions.

Finally, effective coaches must be knowledgeable about the game of football and possess strong strategic and tactical skills. They must be able to develop game plans that play to their team's strengths and weaknesses, and make adjustments on the fly when necessary.

Greatest Coaches in NFL History

1. Vince Lombardi: Vince Lombardi is widely regarded as one of the greatest coaches in NFL history. He coached the Green Bay Packers in the 1960s, leading them to five NFL championships and two Super Bowl victories. Lombardi was known for his strong leadership and motivational skills, and his emphasis on discipline and hard work.

2. Bill Belichick: Bill Belichick is the current head coach of the New England Patriots, and is considered one of the most successful coaches in NFL history. He has led the Patriots to nine Super Bowl appearances and six victories, and is known for his strategic and tactical expertise.

3. Don Shula: Don Shula coached in the NFL for over 30 years, leading the Miami Dolphins to two Super Bowl victories and setting the record for most career wins by a head coach. He was known for his attention to detail and his ability to motivate his players.

4. Chuck Noll: Chuck Noll coached the Pittsburgh Steelers in the 1970s, leading them to four Super Bowl victories in six years. He was known for his ability to develop young talent and his emphasis on teamwork and discipline.

5. Tom Landry: Tom Landry coached the Dallas Cowboys for 29 years, leading them to two Super Bowl victories and five NFC championships. He was known for his strategic and tactical expertise, and his ability to adapt his game plans to his team's strengths and weaknesses.

Importance of Coaching and Team Management

Coaching and team management are critical components of success in American football. Effective coaches and team managers can help build a positive team culture, develop game plans that play to their team's strengths, and provide guidance and feedback to their players.

Coaching and team management can also have a significant impact on the mental and emotional well-being of players. A supportive and positive coaching staff can help players develop confidence and resilience, and can help them perform at their best on the field.

Roles and responsibilities

Roles and responsibilities are an integral part of success in American football. Below we will we will explore the different roles and responsibilities of players on offense and defense, as well as special teams.

Offensive Roles and Responsibilities

1. Quarterback: The quarterback is the leader of the offense, responsible for calling plays, reading the defense, and making decisions about where to throw the ball.

2. Running Back: The running back is responsible for carrying the ball and gaining yardage on the ground. They must be able to run with power and speed, as well as catch passes out of the backfield.

3. Wide Receiver: The wide receiver is responsible for catching passes and gaining yardage through the air. They must be able to run precise routes, make difficult catches, and avoid being tackled by defenders.

4. Tight End: The tight end is responsible for both catching passes and blocking for the running back or quarterback. They must be able to run routes, catch passes, and also block effectively.

5. Offensive Linemen: The offensive linemen are responsible for protecting the quarterback and creating running lanes for the running back. They must work together as a unit to keep defenders away from the quarterback and open up holes for the running back.

Defensive Roles and Responsibilities

6. Defensive Linemen: The defensive linemen are responsible for stopping the run and rushing the quarterback. They must be able to shed blocks and tackle the ball carrier, as well as apply pressure to the quarterback and disrupt the passing game.

7. Linebackers: Linebackers are responsible for stopping the run, covering receivers, and rushing the quarterback. They must be versatile and able to perform multiple roles on the field.

8. Defensive Backs: The defensive backs are responsible for covering the wide receivers and preventing them from catching passes. They must be able to stay with the receiver, make tackles, and also intercept passes.

Special Teams Roles and Responsibilities

9. Kickers and Punters: Kickers and punters are responsible for kicking the ball on field goal attempts, kickoffs, and punts. They must be accurate and have a strong leg, as well as be able to handle the pressure of kicking in critical moments.

10. Return Specialists: Return specialists are responsible for returning kickoffs and punts for yardage. They must be able to avoid defenders and find open space to gain yardage.

11. Long Snappers and Coverage Units: Long snappers are responsible for snapping the ball to the punter or holder for field goal and extra point attempts, while coverage units are responsible for preventing the opposing team's return specialist from gaining yardage or scoring a touchdown.

Importance of Roles and Responsibilities

Roles and responsibilities are critical to the success of a football team. Each player must understand their role and be able to execute their responsibilities effectively. A breakdown in communication or a failure to perform a specific role can have a significant impact on the outcome of a game.

Effective roles and responsibilities also enable teams to work together cohesively and efficiently. When each player understands their role and performs their responsibilities effectively, the team can operate as a well-oiled machine and achieve success on the field.

In conclusion, roles and responsibilities are an essential part of success in American football. Each player has a specific role and responsibility on offense, defense, and special teams, and must be able to execute those responsibilities effectively. Understanding and executing roles and responsibilities is critical to achieving success on the field, and effective teamwork and communication are key to achieving this.

Offensive and defensive coordinators

In American football, the roles of offensive and defensive coordinators are critical to the success of a team. These coordinators are responsible for developing strategies and game plans, coordinating practices and workouts, and making personnel decisions to ensure their team is competitive and capable of winning games. Below we will we will explore the roles and responsibilities of offensive and defensive coordinators and their impact on the success of a team.

Offensive Coordinator

The offensive coordinator is responsible for developing strategies and game plans that maximize the offensive capabilities of the team. This includes developing a playbook of offensive plays, identifying the strengths and weaknesses of individual players and positions, and selecting plays that optimize the talents of the players on the field.

The offensive coordinator works closely with the quarterback, who is the leader of the offense, to develop and execute game plans. This includes analyzing the opposing team's defense and developing a game plan to exploit any weaknesses that are identified. The offensive coordinator must also make in-game adjustments as necessary, based on the performance of the team and the opposing defense.

In addition to developing game plans, the offensive coordinator is also responsible for managing the offensive coaching staff. This includes coordinating practices and workouts, assigning coaching duties, and providing feedback and guidance to coaches and players.

Defensive Coordinator

The defensive coordinator is responsible for developing strategies and game plans that maximize the defensive capabilities of the team. This includes analyzing the opposing team's offensive plays and identifying the strengths and weaknesses of individual players and positions. The defensive coordinator then selects defensive plays that will counteract the opposing team's offensive strengths and exploit any weaknesses that are identified.

The defensive coordinator works closely with the head coach and other members of the coaching staff to develop and execute game plans. This includes analyzing game film and data to identify the strengths and weaknesses of the opposing team's offense and developing strategies to stop them.

In addition to developing game plans, the defensive coordinator is also responsible for managing the defensive coaching staff. This includes coordinating practices and workouts, assigning coaching duties, and providing feedback and guidance to coaches and players.

Impact on Team Success

The role of the offensive and defensive coordinators is critical to the success of a football team. The ability to develop effective strategies and game plans that maximize the strengths of individual players and positions is essential for a team to be competitive and successful.

Effective coordinators must also be able to adjust their strategies and game plans in response to the performance of the team and the opposing team. This requires a deep understanding of the game of football, the strengths and weaknesses of individual players, and the ability to make quick decisions based on game situations.

The success of a team also depends on the ability of the coordinators to communicate effectively with their coaching staff and players. This requires strong leadership skills, the ability to motivate players and coaches, and the ability to provide feedback and guidance in a constructive and positive manner.

In addition to developing effective strategies and game plans, the coordinators must also be able to manage the workload of their coaching staff and players. This includes coordinating practices and workouts, assigning coaching duties, and ensuring that players are prepared and ready for game day.

In conclusion, the roles of offensive and defensive coordinators are critical to the success of a football team. These coordinators are responsible for developing effective strategies and game plans, coordinating practices and workouts, and managing the workload of their coaching staff and players. The success of a team depends on the ability of these coordinators to communicate effectively, make quick decisions, and adjust their strategies in response to game situations. Effective coordination and leadership can make a significant impact on the success of a football team.

Successful coaches and their strategies

In American football, successful coaches are often defined by their ability to develop effective strategies, motivate their players, and make critical decisions in high-pressure situations. Below we will we will explore some of the most successful coaches in football history and the strategies they employed to achieve success.

Vince Lombardi

1. Vince Lombardi is widely regarded as one of the most successful coaches in football history. Lombardi's strategy was simple: focus on the fundamentals and work harder than anyone else. He was a strict disciplinarian who demanded perfection from his players.

Lombardi's coaching philosophy was based on the belief that success comes from hard work, attention to detail, and teamwork. He emphasized the importance of the running game and a strong defense, and he believed that the key to winning was to outwork the opposition.

Lombardi's success with the Green Bay Packers in the 1960s is legendary, with his team winning five NFL championships and two Super Bowls in a span of seven years. Lombardi's focus on the fundamentals and his unwavering commitment to hard work and discipline are still respected and emulated by coaches today.

Bill Belichick

Bill Belichick, the head coach of the New England Patriots, is one of the most successful coaches in football history. Belichick's strategy is based on careful planning and attention to detail. He is known for his meticulous preparation, and he spends countless hours studying film and analyzing his opponents.

Belichick is also known for his ability to adapt to different situations and make critical decisions in high-pressure situations. He is a master of game-day strategy, and he is known for making adjustments on the fly to counteract his opponent's strengths.

Belichick's success with the Patriots is impressive, with the team winning six Super Bowl championships under his leadership. His focus on preparation, attention to detail, and adaptability are key factors in his success as a coach.

Tom Landry

Tom Landry, the legendary coach of the Dallas Cowboys, is known for his innovative strategies and his ability to motivate his players. Landry was a master of the 4-3 defense, which he developed to counteract the running game of opposing teams.

Landry was also a master of the mental game, and he believed that a positive mindset was essential for success. He emphasized the importance of teamwork and hard work, and he was known for his ability to motivate his players to give their best effort.

Under Landry's leadership, the Cowboys won two Super Bowl championships, and his innovative strategies and motivational techniques have influenced coaches and players for decades.

In conclusion, successful coaches in American football share a commitment to hard work, attention to detail, and a willingness to adapt to different situations. Coaches like Vince Lombardi, Bill Belichick, and Tom Landry are known for their innovative strategies and their ability to motivate their players to give their best effort.

The key to success in football is not just about having the best players or the most talented team, but about having a coach who can bring out the best in their players and develop effective strategies that capitalize on the strengths of the team. By studying the strategies of successful coaches, coaches and players can learn valuable lessons that can help them achieve their goals and become successful in their own right.

Strength and Conditioning

Strength and conditioning is a critical component of success in American football. Football is a physically demanding sport that requires players to be strong, fast, and agile. Below we will we will explore the importance of strength and conditioning in football, the types of exercises used in football training, and the impact of strength and conditioning on player performance.

Importance of Strength and Conditioning

Strength and conditioning is important in football for several reasons. First, it helps players develop the strength, power, and endurance they need to perform at a high level. Football players must be able to run, jump, tackle, and block, and they must be able to do so for extended periods of time. Strength and conditioning programs help players develop the physical qualities necessary to excel in these areas.

Second, strength and conditioning can help prevent injuries. Football is a high-contact sport, and injuries are common. A well-designed strength and conditioning program can help players develop the strength and flexibility they need to withstand the physical demands of the sport.

Third, strength and conditioning can help players recover from injuries more quickly. A strong, well-conditioned body is better able to recover from injuries than a weak, poorly-conditioned body. By developing a strong foundation of strength and conditioning, players can reduce the risk of reinjury and get back on the field more quickly.

Types of Exercises Used in Football Training

Strength and conditioning programs for football typically include a combination of exercises designed to develop strength, power, speed, agility, and endurance. These exercises include:

1. Weightlifting: Football players typically use weightlifting exercises to develop overall strength and power. These exercises include squats, deadlifts, bench press, and power cleans.

2. Plyometrics: Plyometric exercises are designed to develop explosive power and speed. These exercises include box jumps, depth jumps, and hurdle jumps.

3. Speed and agility drills: Speed and agility drills are designed to help players develop the footwork and quickness they need to move quickly and change direction on the field. These drills include ladder drills, cone drills, and agility hurdles.

4. Cardiovascular training: Cardiovascular training is important for developing endurance and stamina. Football players typically use running and sprinting exercises to develop cardiovascular fitness.

Impact of Strength and Conditioning on Player Performance

The impact of strength and conditioning on player performance in football is significant. A well-designed strength and conditioning program can help players develop the physical qualities they need to perform at a high level. This includes developing strength, power, speed, agility, and endurance.

Stronger players are better able to block, tackle, and run with the ball. More powerful players can generate more force with their movements, which can help them break tackles and gain yards. Faster, more agile players are better able to change direction quickly and evade defenders. Endurance training can help players maintain their performance over the course of a long game or season.

In addition to improving physical performance, strength and conditioning can also have a positive impact on mental performance. Players who are well-conditioned and physically fit are better able to focus and concentrate on the game. They are also more confident in their abilities, which can help them perform better under pressure.

In conclusion, strength and conditioning is a critical component of success in American football. Strength and conditioning programs help players develop the physical qualities they need to perform at a high level, prevent injuries, and recover more quickly from injuries. These programs typically include a combination of weightlifting, plyometrics, speed and agility drills, and cardiovascular training. The impact of strength and conditioning on player performance is significant, and coaches and players alike should prioritize this aspect of their training in order to excel on the field.

Training programs and workouts

Training programs and workouts are an essential part of American football. These programs are designed to help players develop the strength, speed, and agility they need to excel on the field. Below we will we will explore the different types of training programs and workouts used in football, and the benefits of each.

Types of Training Programs

1. Off-Season Training: Off-season training is typically conducted during the period between the end of one season and the start of the next. During this time, players focus on developing overall strength and conditioning, as well as improving specific areas of weakness. Off-season training typically involves weightlifting, plyometrics, speed and agility drills, and cardiovascular training.

2. Pre-Season Training: Pre-season training is designed to help players prepare for the upcoming season. During this time, players focus on developing their football-specific skills, such as blocking, tackling, and running routes. Pre-season training typically involves a combination of on-field drills and weightlifting.

3. In-Season Training: In-season training is designed to help players maintain their fitness and performance throughout the season. This type of training typically involves lighter weightlifting and maintenance of cardiovascular fitness.

Types of Workouts

4. Weightlifting: Weightlifting is a critical component of football training. It helps players develop overall strength and power, which is important for blocking, tackling, and running with the ball. Weightlifting exercises include squats, deadlifts, bench press, and power cleans.

5. Plyometrics: Plyometric exercises are designed to help players develop explosive power and speed. These exercises include box jumps, depth jumps, and hurdle jumps.

6. Speed and Agility Drills: Speed and agility drills are designed to help players develop the footwork and quickness they need to move quickly and change direction on the field. These drills include ladder drills, cone drills, and agility hurdles.

7. Cardiovascular Training: Cardiovascular training is important for developing endurance and stamina. Football players typically use running and sprinting exercises to develop cardiovascular fitness.

Benefits of Training Programs and Workouts

8. Improved Strength and Power: Training programs and workouts help players develop the strength and power they need to perform at a high level on the field. This includes blocking, tackling, and running with the ball.

9. Improved Speed and Agility: Speed and agility are critical components of football performance. Training programs and workouts help players develop the footwork and quickness they need to move quickly and change direction on the field.

10. Injury Prevention: Training programs and workouts can help prevent injuries by improving overall strength and conditioning. A well-conditioned body is better able to withstand the physical demands of football.

11. Improved Mental Performance: Training programs and workouts can also have a positive impact on mental performance. Players who are well-conditioned and physically fit are better able to focus and concentrate on the game. They are also more confident in their abilities, which can help them perform better under pressure.

In conclusion, training programs and workouts are an essential component of success in American football. These programs help players develop the strength, speed, and agility they need to perform at a high level on the field, as well as prevent injuries and improve mental performance. Coaches and players should prioritize training programs and workouts in order to achieve their full potential and excel on the football field.

Nutrition and recovery

Nutrition and recovery are two critical components of success in American football. The physical demands of the sport require players to be strong, fast, and agile, and they must be able to perform at a high level for extended periods of time. Below we will we will explore the importance of nutrition and recovery in football, the types of foods and supplements used by players, and the impact of nutrition and recovery on player performance.

Importance of Nutrition and Recovery

Nutrition and recovery are important in football for several reasons. First, proper nutrition is essential for developing and maintaining the strength and endurance needed to perform at a high level. Football players require a high-calorie, high-protein diet to support their physical activity.

Second, recovery is critical for preventing injuries and promoting overall health. Football players need to get enough sleep, rest, and recovery time to allow their bodies to heal and repair after the physical demands of training and games.

Types of Foods and Supplements

1. Protein: Protein is critical for muscle growth and repair. Football players typically consume protein-rich foods such as chicken, fish, beef, and eggs. They may also use protein supplements such as whey protein powder.

2. Carbohydrates: Carbohydrates are an important source of energy for football players. They provide the fuel needed for intense physical activity. Football players typically consume carbohydrates from sources such as whole grains, fruits, and vegetables.

3. Fats: Fats are important for maintaining overall health, but should be consumed in moderation. Football players typically consume healthy fats from sources such as nuts, seeds, and olive oil.

4. Hydration: Hydration is critical for overall health and athletic performance. Football players need to consume plenty of water and electrolytes to prevent dehydration.

Impact of Nutrition and Recovery on Player Performance

The impact of nutrition and recovery on player performance in football is significant. Proper nutrition helps players develop the physical qualities they need to perform at a high level. This includes developing strength, endurance, and speed.

Recovery is critical for preventing injuries and promoting overall health. Players who get enough sleep, rest, and recovery time are better able to perform at a high level and avoid injuries. Additionally, proper nutrition and recovery can help players recover more quickly from injuries, allowing them to get back on the field more quickly.

In addition to improving physical performance, nutrition and recovery can also have a positive impact on mental performance. Players who are well-nourished and well-rested are better able to focus and concentrate on the game. They are also more confident in their abilities, which can help them perform better under pressure.

In conclusion, nutrition and recovery are critical components of success in American football. Proper nutrition provides the fuel needed to develop and maintain the physical qualities required for high-level performance. Recovery is critical for preventing injuries and promoting overall health. Football players should prioritize nutrition and recovery in their training programs in order to achieve their full potential and excel on the field.

Injury prevention

Injury prevention is an important aspect of American football. Due to the physical nature of the sport, football players are at risk of sustaining injuries, some of which can be severe and have long-lasting effects on their health and performance. Below we will we will explore the importance of injury prevention in football, the types of injuries that players are at risk for, and the strategies and techniques used to prevent injuries.

Importance of Injury Prevention

Injury prevention is critical in football for several reasons. First, injuries can have a significant impact on a player's performance and overall health. An injury can cause a player to miss games or even entire seasons, which can negatively impact their career trajectory.

Second, injuries can also have long-lasting effects on a player's health and well-being. Repeated concussions and other traumatic injuries can lead to chronic health problems such as memory loss and mood disorders.

Types of Injuries

Football players are at risk for a variety of injuries, including:

1. Concussions: Concussions are a common injury in football. They occur when a player's head is hit hard enough to cause the brain to move inside the skull. Concussions can have long-lasting effects on a player's health, including memory loss and mood disorders.

2. Ligament injuries: Ligament injuries, such as ACL and MCL tears, are also common in football. These injuries occur when a player's knee twists or turns in an awkward position, causing damage to the ligaments.

3. Fractures: Fractures are another common injury in football. They occur when a player's bone breaks due to the force of a hit or fall.

Strategies and Techniques for Injury Prevention

4. Proper Equipment: Wearing proper equipment is critical for preventing injuries in football. This includes helmets, shoulder pads, knee pads, and mouthguards. Equipment should be properly fitted and maintained to ensure that it provides adequate protection.

5. Proper Technique: Proper technique is important for preventing injuries in football. Players should be taught proper tackling, blocking, and other football-specific techniques to minimize the risk of injury.

6. Strength and Conditioning: Strength and conditioning are critical for preventing injuries in football. A well-conditioned body is better able to withstand the physical demands of the sport, and can better absorb the force of hits and falls.

7. Warm-Up and Cool-Down: Proper warm-up and cool-down routines are important for preventing injuries. Players should engage in a dynamic warm-up before practice or games to prepare their bodies for physical activity, and a static cool-down afterwards to promote recovery and reduce the risk of injury.

8. Rest and Recovery: Rest and recovery are important for preventing injuries in football. Players should get enough sleep and rest, and allow their bodies time to recover between games and practices.

Injury prevention is an important aspect of American football. Proper equipment, technique, strength and conditioning, warm-up and cool-down routines, and rest and recovery are all critical for preventing injuries in football. Coaches and players should prioritize injury prevention in their training programs and on-field practices to ensure that players are able to perform at a high level while minimizing the risk of injury.

Developing Football Skills

Developing football skills is a critical aspect of success in American football. Football players require a range of physical and technical skills in order to perform at a high level, including strength, speed, agility, and coordination. Below we will we will explore the importance of developing football skills, the types of skills required for success in football, and the strategies and techniques used to develop these skills.

Importance of Developing Football Skills

Developing football skills is important for several reasons. First, proper technique is critical for preventing injuries and maximizing performance. Players who are taught proper tackling, blocking, and other football-specific techniques are better able to avoid injuries and perform at a high level.

Second, developing football skills is important for building confidence and improving mental performance. Players who are well-versed in the skills required for their position are better able to focus and concentrate on the game. They are also more confident in their abilities, which can help them perform better under pressure.

Types of Skills Required for Success in Football

Football players require a range of skills in order to perform at a high level. These include:

1. Physical Skills: Physical skills such as strength, speed, agility, and coordination are critical for success in football. These skills are developed through strength and conditioning programs, as well as drills and exercises designed to improve speed, agility, and coordination.

2. Technical Skills: Technical skills such as tackling, blocking, catching, and throwing are also critical for success in football. These skills are developed through drills and exercises designed to improve technique and performance.

3. Mental Skills: Mental skills such as focus, concentration, and confidence are also important for success in football. These skills can be developed through visualization exercises, positive self-talk, and other mental training techniques.

Strategies and Techniques for Developing Football Skills

4. Practice: Practice is critical for developing football skills. Players should engage in regular practice sessions to build their physical and technical skills. Practice should be focused and structured, with a clear set of goals and objectives.

5. Drills and Exercises: Drills and exercises are important for developing football skills. These should be designed to improve technique and performance, and should be tailored to the individual needs of each player.

6. Coaching: Coaching is critical for developing football skills. Coaches should provide guidance and feedback to help players improve their technique and performance. They should also provide motivation and support to help players develop confidence and mental toughness.

7. Strength and Conditioning Programs: Strength and conditioning programs are important for developing physical skills in football. These programs should be designed to improve strength, speed, agility, and coordination, and should be tailored to the individual needs of each player.

8. Mental Training: Mental training is important for developing mental skills in football. Players should engage in visualization exercises, positive self-talk, and other mental training techniques to improve focus, concentration, and confidence.

In conclusion, developing football skills is critical for success in American football. Physical skills, technical skills, and mental skills are all important for performing at a high level. Strategies and techniques such as practice, drills and exercises, coaching, strength and conditioning programs, and mental training can all be used to develop these skills. Coaches and players should prioritize skill development in their training programs in order to achieve their full potential and excel on the field.

Drills and practice routines

Drills and practice routines are essential for developing the physical and technical skills required for success in American football. Football players must be proficient in a wide range of skills, including tackling, blocking, catching, throwing, and running. Below we will we will explore the importance of drills and practice routines in football, the types of drills and routines used to develop skills, and how to design effective practice sessions.

Importance of Drills and Practice Routines

Drills and practice routines are critical for developing the skills necessary for success in football. These activities help players to improve their technique, build strength and conditioning, and develop mental toughness. They also provide opportunities for players to work on specific aspects of their game and to focus on areas that need improvement.

Types of Drills and Routines

There are many different types of drills and routines used in football. Some of the most common include:

1. Individual Drills: Individual drills focus on improving specific skills for individual players. These drills may include catching, throwing, tackling, or blocking. They are designed to help players improve their technique and to build their confidence.

2. Group Drills: Group drills involve multiple players and are designed to improve teamwork and coordination. These drills may include passing or running drills, and are used to develop communication and coordination between players.

3. Conditioning Drills: Conditioning drills are used to build strength and endurance. These drills may include running, jumping, or weightlifting exercises.

4. Scrimmages: Scrimmages are used to simulate game situations and provide players with the opportunity to practice their skills in a real game setting. Scrimmages are also used to help coaches evaluate players and to make adjustments to their strategies and tactics.

Designing Effective Practice Sessions

To design effective practice sessions, coaches should consider the needs of their players and the goals they want to achieve. This may involve identifying areas where players need improvement and designing drills and routines that target these areas. It may also involve adjusting the intensity and duration of practice sessions to ensure that players are able to build their strength and endurance without becoming fatigued or injured.

Coaches should also consider the use of feedback and evaluation to help players improve their technique and performance. This may involve providing feedback on specific aspects of a player's performance, or using video analysis to help players identify areas where they need to improve.

In conclusion, drills and practice routines are essential for developing the physical and technical skills required for success in American football. Coaches and players should prioritize skill development in their training programs and design effective practice sessions that target specific areas of need. By focusing on the development of individual skills, teamwork, conditioning, and game simulation, coaches can help their players achieve their full potential and excel on the field.

Mental preparation and focus

Mental preparation and focus are critical components of success in American football. Football players must not only be physically fit, but also mentally prepared and focused in order to perform at their best. Below we will we will explore the importance of mental preparation and focus in football, the strategies and techniques used to develop these skills, and the benefits of mental preparation and focus on performance.

Importance of Mental Preparation and Focus

Mental preparation and focus are important for several reasons. First, they help players to perform at their best under pressure. Football games are high-stakes events that require players to perform at their best even when they are feeling nervous or distracted. Mental preparation and focus can help players to stay calm and focused in these situations, which can improve their performance.

Second, mental preparation and focus can help players to improve their confidence and self-belief. When players are mentally prepared and focused, they are more likely to believe in themselves and their abilities. This can help them to perform at their best and to achieve their goals.

Strategies and Techniques for Mental Preparation and Focus

There are several strategies and techniques that football players can use to develop their mental preparation and focus. These include:

1. Visualization: Visualization involves imagining a positive outcome in a specific situation. Football players can use visualization to prepare mentally for specific game situations, such as making a game-winning touchdown or intercepting a pass.

2. Positive Self-Talk: Positive self-talk involves using positive statements to build confidence and self-belief. Football players can use positive self-talk to build their confidence and to stay focused on their goals.

3. Breathing Techniques: Breathing techniques can help football players to stay calm and focused under pressure. Techniques such as deep breathing and visualization can help players to reduce stress and anxiety and to improve their focus.

4. Mindfulness: Mindfulness involves focusing on the present moment and being aware of one's thoughts and emotions. Football players can use mindfulness techniques to stay focused on the task at hand and to reduce distractions.

Benefits of Mental Preparation and Focus on Performance

Mental preparation and focus can have several benefits on performance in American football. These include:

5. Improved Performance: When players are mentally prepared and focused, they are more likely to perform at their best. They are less likely to be distracted by negative thoughts or emotions, and they are more likely to stay focused on the task at hand.

6. Improved Confidence: Mental preparation and focus can also improve players' confidence and self-belief. When players believe in themselves and their abilities, they are more likely to perform at their best and to achieve their goals.

7. Improved Resilience: Mental preparation and focus can also improve players' resilience in the face of adversity. When players are mentally prepared and focused, they are better able to bounce back from setbacks and to stay focused on their goals.

In conclusion, mental preparation and focus are critical components of success in American football. Football players must not only be physically fit, but also mentally prepared and focused in order to perform at their best. Strategies and techniques such as visualization, positive self-talk, breathing techniques, and mindfulness can help players to develop their mental preparation and focus. By improving their mental preparation and focus, football players can improve their performance, confidence, and resilience on the field.

Learning from the pros

Learning from the pros is an important aspect of developing as a football player. Professional football players have years of experience and have mastered the technical and mental skills necessary to succeed at the highest level. By studying and learning from the pros, football players at all levels can improve their own skills and performance. Below we will we will explore the benefits of learning from the pros, the ways in which football players can learn from the pros, and the strategies and techniques used by professional football players.

Benefits of Learning from the Pros

There are several benefits to learning from the pros in football. These include:

1. Learning Technical Skills: Professional football players have mastered the technical skills necessary to succeed at the highest level. By studying the techniques and strategies used by professional players, football players at all levels can improve their own skills.

2. Learning Mental Skills: Professional football players also have strong mental skills, including focus, resilience, and confidence. By studying the mental preparation and focus of professional players, football players can improve their own mental toughness.

3. Learning from Experience: Professional football players have years of experience playing at the highest level. By studying their experiences, football players can gain insights into the challenges and opportunities they will face on the field.

Ways to Learn from the Pros

There are several ways in which football players can learn from the pros. These include:

4. Watching Games: Watching professional football games is a great way to learn from the pros. By watching how professional players move on the field, how they react to different situations, and how they work with their teammates, football players can gain insights into the strategies and techniques used by professional players.

5. Studying Game Film: Game film is a valuable tool for studying the techniques and strategies used by professional players. By watching game film, football players can see how professional players react to different situations and how they use their skills to succeed on the field.

6. Attending Clinics and Workshops: Attending clinics and workshops hosted by professional football players is a great way to learn from the pros. These events provide opportunities for football players to meet and learn from professional players and to gain insights into their techniques and strategies.

Strategies and Techniques Used by Professional Football Players

Professional football players use a wide range of strategies and techniques to succeed on the field. These include:

7. Technical Skills: Professional football players have mastered a wide range of technical skills, including passing, blocking, tackling, and running. They have spent years practicing and refining these skills in order to perform at the highest level.

8. Mental Preparation: Professional football players also have strong mental skills, including focus, resilience, and confidence. They use visualization, positive self-talk, and other techniques to prepare mentally for games and to stay focused on their goals.

9. Teamwork: Professional football players work closely with their teammates to achieve success on the field. They communicate effectively, support each other, and work together to overcome challenges and obstacles.

In conclusion, learning from the pros is an important aspect of developing as a football player. By studying the techniques and strategies used by professional players, football players at all levels can improve their own skills and performance. Watching games, studying game film, and attending clinics and workshops are all great ways to learn from the pros. By mastering technical and mental skills and working closely with their teammates, professional football players have achieved success at the highest level. By learning from their experiences, football players at all levels can achieve their own goals and succeed on the field.

College Football

College football is a popular and exciting sport in the United States. Every year, millions of fans across the country tune in to watch their favorite college teams compete on the field. Below we will we will explore the history and development of college football, the current landscape of college football, and the impact of college football on American culture.

History and Development of College Football

College football has a rich and storied history. The first college football game was played in 1869 between Rutgers and Princeton. Over the years, college football grew in popularity, and by the early 20th century, it had become one of the most popular sports in America.

In the 1920s and 1930s, college football underwent significant changes. The introduction of the forward pass and other rule changes made the game more exciting and high-scoring. College football also became more organized during this time, with the establishment of regional conferences and bowl games.

The current landscape of College Football

Today, college football is played at over 700 schools across the country. The National Collegiate Athletic Association (NCAA) governs college football, and teams are divided into three divisions based on size and resources. Division I is the highest level of college football, and includes the most well-known and prestigious programs.

The college football season typically runs from late August to early January, with the highlight being the College Football Playoff. The College Football Playoff consists of four teams selected by a committee and culminates in the National Championship game.

Impact of College Football on American Culture

College football has had a significant impact on American culture. It is deeply embedded in the traditions and identity of many universities and communities across the country. The game brings together people of all backgrounds and creates a sense of community and camaraderie.

College football also generates a significant amount of revenue for universities and the NCAA. The popularity of college football has led to lucrative television contracts, sponsorships, and ticket sales.

However, college football has also faced criticism in recent years. There are concerns about the safety and well-being of student-athletes, particularly regarding head injuries and long-term health effects. There have also been debates about whether student-athletes should be paid for their participation in college sports.

In conclusion, college football is a popular and exciting sport with a rich history and significant impact on American culture. It brings together communities and generates significant revenue for universities and the NCAA. However, college football also faces challenges and debates about the safety and well-being of student-athletes and the compensation they receive. Despite these challenges, college football remains a beloved and iconic part of American sports culture.

History and traditions

Football is a game that has a rich history and is steeped in tradition. From the early days of the game to the modern era, football has evolved and changed, yet many of the traditions and customs that have defined the game for generations continue to endure. Below we will we will explore the history and traditions of football, including its roots in ancient sports, the development of modern football, and the customs and practices that make the game unique.

Ancient Roots of Football

Football has its roots in ancient sports that were played in different parts of the world. For example, the ancient Greeks played a game called harpastum, which involved two teams trying to move a ball across a boundary line. In China, a game called cuju was played, which involved kicking a ball through a goalpost. These early games had similarities to modern football, such as using a ball and trying to score points, but they were played with different rules and had different objectives.

Development of Modern Football

The game of football as we know it today was developed in England during the 19th century. In the early years, different clubs had their own rules, but over time, a standardized set of rules was established. In 1863, the Football Association was founded, and it became the governing body for football in England.

1. Football quickly spread to other parts of the world, and by the early 20th century, it had become a popular sport in Europe, South America, and North America. The sport continued to evolve, with new rules and strategies being developed, but the basic objective of the game remained the same: to score more points than the other team.

Customs and Practices

Football has a number of customs and practices that are unique to the game. These traditions have evolved over time and are an important part of the sport's history and culture.

One of the most important traditions in football is the pregame ritual. Before the game, players from both teams typically take the field for warmups, and then the teams line up to shake hands with each other. This is a sign of respect and sportsmanship, and it is a tradition that has been carried on for many years.

Another important tradition in football is the halftime show. At halftime, the marching band typically performs a show for the crowd, and sometimes there are special guests or performers. The halftime show is an important part of the game-day experience and has become a staple of football games.

Other traditions in football include tailgating, where fans gather in the parking lot before the game to eat, drink, and socialize; the coin toss, where the captains of both teams determine who will start with the ball; and the victory formation, where the winning team takes a knee to run out the clock and secure the win.

In conclusion, football is a game with a rich history and deep traditions. From its roots in ancient sports to the modern game played today, football has evolved and changed, but many of the customs and practices that define the sport have endured. These traditions are an important part of football's culture and history, and they help to make the game unique and special.

NCAA conferences and rivalries

The NCAA, or National Collegiate Athletic Association, is the governing body for college sports in the United States. College football is one of the most popular sports in the country, and it is played at over 700 schools across the nation. These schools are divided into conferences based on geography, and each conference has its own set of teams and rivalries. Below we will we will explore the NCAA conferences and rivalries that make college football such an exciting and unique sport.

NCAA Conferences

The NCAA has three divisions for college sports, with Division I being the highest level. Within Division I, there are 10 conferences, each with their own set of teams and rules. The conferences are:

ACC (Atlantic Coast Conference)

Big 12

Big Ten

Conference USA

Independents

MAC (Mid-American Conference)

Mountain West

PAC-12 (Pacific-12 Conference)

SEC (Southeastern Conference)

Sun Belt

Each conference has a commissioner and a set of rules and regulations that govern its teams. The conferences also have their own championship games at the end of the season, which determine the conference champion and sometimes influence the College Football Playoff selection process.

Rivalries

College football is known for its intense rivalries between teams, which often have deep historical roots. Rivalries can develop for many reasons, such as geographic proximity, shared history, or intense competition.

Some of the most well-known rivalries in college football include:

Alabama vs. Auburn (Iron Bowl)

Michigan vs. Ohio State (The Game)

USC vs. UCLA (The Battle for LA)

Army vs. Navy (Army-Navy Game)

Oklahoma vs. Texas (Red River Rivalry)

These rivalries often bring out the best in both teams, and they are highly anticipated events each season. Some rivalries also have unique traditions associated with them, such as the Alabama vs. Auburn Iron Bowl trophy, which is a cast-iron statue of a football player.

Impact on College Football

The NCAA conferences and rivalries are an integral part of the college football experience. They create a sense of identity and community for fans, players, and coaches, and they contribute to the excitement and drama of the game.

Conference play is an important part of the college football season, and it often determines which teams will advance to the conference championship games and the College Football Playoff. Rivalries also add an extra level of intensity and excitement to the game, and they often attract national attention and media coverage.

In conclusion, the NCAA conferences and rivalries are an important part of the college football experience. They create a sense of identity and community for fans and players, and they contribute to the excitement and drama of the game. The conferences and rivalries also play a significant role in determining which teams will advance to the College Football Playoff and other postseason events. College football is a unique and exciting sport, and the conferences and rivalries are a major reason why.

Recruiting and scholarships

Recruiting and scholarships are two essential components of the college football experience. They are also among the most important aspects of building a successful program. Below we will we will explore the recruiting and scholarship processes, and how they impact college football.

Recruiting Process

Recruiting is the process by which colleges and universities identify and attract talented high school football players to their programs. The process can be lengthy and competitive, with many schools vying for the same players.

Recruiting typically begins in a player's junior year of high school, when coaches can begin contacting them directly. Coaches may attend high school games, watch game film, and speak with high school coaches to evaluate potential recruits.

Once a player has been identified as a potential recruit, coaches will typically invite them to visit the campus for an official visit. During the visit, the player will meet with coaches, tour the facilities, and meet current players. The goal of the visit is to convince the player to commit to the program.

If a player decides to commit to a program, they will sign a National Letter of Intent (NLI), which binds them to the school for one year. Once a player has signed an NLI, other schools are no longer allowed to recruit them.

Scholarship Process

Scholarships are financial awards given to student-athletes to cover the cost of attending college. In college football, scholarships are awarded to players who have committed to the program.

Scholarships cover tuition, room and board, and other expenses associated with attending college. They are typically awarded on a yearly basis, and can be renewed for up to four years.

The number of scholarships a school can offer is determined by the NCAA. In Division I, schools are allowed to offer up to 85 scholarships for football.

Scholarship offers are typically made in conjunction with the recruiting process. Coaches will evaluate a player's talent and potential, and offer them a scholarship if they believe they can contribute to the program.

Impact on College Football

Recruiting and scholarships are critical to the success of college football programs. The ability to recruit and sign talented players can make the difference between a winning and losing season.

Scholarships are also important in terms of making college accessible to student-athletes. Many football players come from disadvantaged backgrounds, and without scholarships, they may not have the opportunity to attend college.

Recruiting and scholarships can also impact the competitive balance of college football. Schools with more resources and better recruiting networks may have an advantage over smaller schools. This has led to concerns about the increasing gap between the haves and have-nots in college football.

In conclusion, recruiting and scholarships are essential components of the college football experience. They allow programs to identify and attract talented players, and they provide financial support to student-athletes. The recruiting and scholarship processes can be competitive and intense, with many schools vying for the same players. The impact of recruiting and scholarships on college football cannot be overstated, as they play a critical role in determining which programs are successful and which are not.

The NFL: America's Game

The National Football League, or NFL, is the premier professional football league in the United States. It is the highest level of football in the country, and it is one of the most popular sports leagues in the world. Below we will we will explore the history and significance of the NFL, and why it has become known as America's Game.

History of the NFL

The NFL was founded in 1920 as the American Professional Football Association (APFA). The league consisted of 10 teams, and it was primarily based in the Midwest. Over the years, the league expanded and evolved, and in 1960, the American Football League (AFL) was formed as a rival league.

1. The two leagues competed with each other for several years, but in 1966, they agreed to merge into a single league with two conferences: the AFC and the NFC. The first Super Bowl, which pitted the champions of each conference against each other, was played in 1967.

Since then, the NFL has continued to grow and evolve, with new teams and stadiums being added, and new rules and technologies being introduced. Today, the league consists of 32 teams, and it generates billions of dollars in revenue each year.

Why the NFL is America's Game

The NFL has become known as America's Game for several reasons. First and foremost, it is an incredibly popular and widely watched sport in the United States. Millions of people tune in to watch NFL games each week, and the Super Bowl, which is the championship game of the NFL, is one of the most watched television events in the country.

The NFL is also deeply ingrained in American culture. Football is a beloved pastime that is played and watched by people of all ages, races, and backgrounds. The sport is often associated with traditional American values like hard work, perseverance, and teamwork.

The NFL is also a significant economic force in the United States. The league generates billions of dollars in revenue each year, and it employs thousands of people in a variety of roles, from players and coaches to executives and support staff. The league also has a significant impact on local economies, as NFL games can bring in millions of dollars in tourism and other economic activity.

Finally, the NFL is known for its unique traditions and rituals, which have become a part of American culture. From the Super Bowl halftime show to the Thanksgiving Day games, the NFL has created many memorable moments and traditions that are cherished by fans.

Impact of the NFL

The NFL has had a significant impact on American culture and society. It has provided a platform for athletes to showcase their talent and achieve their dreams, while also providing entertainment and inspiration for millions of fans.

The NFL has also been at the forefront of social and cultural change. Over the years, the league has addressed issues like player safety, domestic violence, and racial equality. The NFL has also been a leader in promoting charitable causes and supporting communities in need.

The NFL has also had a significant impact on the global community. The league has expanded its reach beyond the United States, with games being played in countries like Mexico and the United Kingdom. The NFL has also been involved in international efforts to promote the sport, and it has helped to develop the game in other countries.

In conclusion, the NFL is a beloved and significant part of American culture. It is a source of entertainment, inspiration, and tradition for millions of people, and it has had a significant impact on American society and the world. The NFL's popularity and influence have made it a symbol of American values and culture, and it is likely to continue to be America's Game for years to come.

League structure and history

The National Football League (NFL) is the premier professional football league in the United States, with a long and rich history that dates back nearly a century. Below we will we will explore the league's structure, its history, and some of the key milestones and events that have shaped the NFL into what it is today.

League Structure

1. The NFL is divided into two conferences: the American Football Conference (AFC) and the National Football Conference (NFC). Each conference is further divided into four divisions: North, South, East, and West. Each division has four teams, for a total of 32 teams in the league.

The NFL regular season consists of 17 weeks, with each team playing 16 games and having one bye week. At the end of the regular season, the top six teams from each conference advance to the playoffs. The playoffs consist of four rounds, culminating in the Super Bowl, which is the championship game of the NFL.

History of the NFL

The NFL was founded in 1920 as the American Professional Football Association (APFA). The league consisted of 10 teams, mostly based in the Midwest. In 1922, the league changed its name to the National Football League (NFL), and it continued to grow and evolve over the years.

2. One of the key events in the history of the NFL was the merger with the American Football League (AFL) in 1970. The two leagues had been competing with each other for several years, but they agreed to merge into a single league with two conferences: the AFC and the NFC. The first Super Bowl, which pitted the champions of each conference against each other, was played in 1967.

Over the years, the NFL has continued to grow and evolve, with new teams and stadiums being added, and new rules and technologies being introduced. The league has also faced several challenges and controversies, including issues related to player safety, domestic violence, and racial equality.

Key Milestones and Events

Throughout its history, the NFL has been marked by many key milestones and events that have shaped the league and the sport of football in general. Some of these include:

3. 1920: Founding of the APFA, which later becomes the NFL

4. 1932: Creation of the first NFL Championship Game

5. 1960: Formation of the American Football League (AFL)

6. 1967: First Super Bowl is played

7. 1970: Merger of the NFL and the AFL

8. 1972: Implementation of the 14-game regular season schedule

9. 1982: Introduction of the "K-Gun" offense by the Buffalo Bills

10. 1985: Formation of the World League of American Football (later renamed NFL Europe)

11. 1987: Implementation of the 3-point stance for offensive linemen

12. 1993: Implementation of free agency

13. 2002: Creation of the AFC and NFC Championship Games

14. 2009: Introduction of the Wild Card round of the playoffs

In conclusion, the NFL is a storied and influential league with a long and rich history. The league has grown and evolved over the years, and it has faced many challenges and controversies along the way. The NFL's structure, with its two conferences and four divisions, has remained relatively consistent over the years, and the league's key milestones and events have shaped the sport of football in profound ways. Today, the NFL continues to be one of the most popular and watched sports leagues in the world, and it is likely to remain a cultural and economic force for years to come.

The draft and free agency

The NFL draft and free agency are two key components of the league's player acquisition system. Below we will we will explore how the draft and free agency work, and how they have evolved over time to become an integral part of the NFL's structure.

The Draft

The NFL draft is an annual event in which teams select new players from a pool of eligible college football players. The draft is typically held in late April or early May, and it lasts for seven rounds. The order of the draft is determined by the previous season's standings, with the team that finished with the worst record selecting first and the Super Bowl champion selecting last.

Each team is allotted a certain number of draft picks based on their position in the draft order. The higher a team's draft position, the more picks they will have. Teams can also trade their draft picks with other teams in order to move up or down in the draft order.

The draft has become a highly anticipated event for football fans, and it is widely covered by the media. Many experts offer their opinions on which players are likely to be drafted in the first round, and fans closely follow their team's picks to see which players they believe will help their team the most.

Free Agency

Free agency is another way for teams to acquire new players. Unlike the draft, which only includes college players, free agency allows teams to sign players who have already played in the NFL. Players become free agents when their contract with their current team expires, or when they are released by their team.

1. There are two types of free agency: unrestricted and restricted. Unrestricted free agents can sign with any team they choose, while restricted free agents can negotiate with other teams, but their current team has the right to match any offer they receive.

The NFL's free agency system was introduced in 1993, and it has since become a key way for teams to improve their rosters. Many teams use free agency to fill gaps in their roster or to acquire players who can make an immediate impact.

Evolution of the Draft and Free Agency

The draft and free agency have both evolved over time to become more complex and nuanced. In the early days of the NFL, there was no draft, and teams were free to sign any player they wanted. This led to a situation where the most talented players would often sign with the same few teams, leaving other teams at a disadvantage.

The draft was introduced in 1936 as a way to level the playing field and ensure that all teams had a chance to acquire the best players. Over time, the draft has become more complex, with teams now able to trade draft picks and use complex strategies to acquire the players they want.

Free agency was introduced in 1993 as a way to give players more control over their careers and to provide teams with another way to acquire talent. Since then, the free agency system has become more complex, with teams now able to use various tools to keep their own players from becoming free agents, such as the franchise tag and transition tag.

The draft and free agency have also had a significant impact on the NFL's competitive balance. The draft ensures that all teams have a chance to acquire top talent, while free agency allows teams to fill gaps in their roster and acquire players who can make an immediate impact.

The draft and free agency are two key components of the NFL's player acquisition system. The draft allows teams to select new players from a pool of college talent, while free agency allows teams to sign players who have already played in the NFL. Both systems have evolved over time to become more complex and nuanced, and they have had a significant impact on the league's competitive balance. With the draft and free agency, teams have a wide range of tools at their disposal to build their rosters and compete for championships.

The road to the Super Bowl

The Super Bowl is the culmination of the NFL season, and it is one of the biggest events in American sports. For the teams that make it to the Super Bowl, the journey is a long and difficult one, full of challenges and obstacles. Below we will we will explore the road to the Super Bowl, from the regular season to the playoffs and beyond.

The Regular Season

The road to the Super Bowl begins in the regular season, which runs from September to December. During the regular season, each team plays 16 games, with the goal of winning as many games as possible and earning a spot in the playoffs. At the end of the regular season, the teams with the best records in each conference qualify for the playoffs.

The Playoffs

1. The playoffs are a single-elimination tournament in which the best teams from each conference compete for the right to play in the Super Bowl. The playoffs begin in early January and consist of three rounds: the Wild Card Round, the Divisional Round, and the Conference Championship.

In the Wild Card Round, the two lowest-seeded teams from each conference play each other, while the top two seeds have a bye. The winners of the Wild Card Round advance to the Divisional Round, where they face the top-seeded teams in each conference.

The winners of the Divisional Round advance to the Conference Championship, where they face off to determine which team will represent their conference in the Super Bowl.

The Super Bowl

The Super Bowl is played on the first Sunday in February, and it is one of the biggest events in American sports. The Super Bowl is more than just a football game – it is a cultural phenomenon, with millions of people tuning in to watch the game and the halftime show.

The Super Bowl is played at a neutral site, and the teams that make it to the game are the best of the best. The game is the culmination of a long and difficult season, and it is the ultimate goal for every NFL team.

The Importance of Momentum

One of the key factors in the road to the Super Bowl is momentum. Teams that are playing well heading into the playoffs are more likely to make a deep run, while teams that are struggling may not make it out of the Wild Card Round.

Momentum can come from a variety of sources, including strong play from the quarterback, a dominant defense, or a hot streak from a particular player. The key is for teams to find a way to build momentum and carry it through the playoffs.

The Importance of Coaching

Another key factor in the road to the Super Bowl is coaching. In the playoffs, coaching can make a huge difference, as coaches must make quick decisions and adjust their game plans on the fly.

Coaches who are able to make the right adjustments and get their players to execute their game plan are more likely to be successful in the playoffs. This is why experienced coaches with a track record of success often do well in the postseason.

The Importance of Team Chemistry

Finally, team chemistry is another key factor in the road to the Super Bowl. Teams that are able to work together and play as a cohesive unit are more likely to succeed in the playoffs.

Chemistry can come from a variety of sources, including strong leadership from the coaching staff and veteran players, as well as a positive team culture. When players trust each other and believe in each other, they are more likely to perform well on the field.

The road to the Super Bowl is a long and difficult one, full of challenges and obstacles. From the regular season to the playoffs and beyond, teams must navigate a complex landscape of opponents, momentum, coaching, and team chemistry in order to reach the ultimate goal. For the teams that make it to the Super Bowl, the journey is a testament to their hard work, determination,

The Greatest Games

Football is a sport that has produced some of the most memorable moments in sports history, and the greatest games are the ones that are still talked about years later. These games are not only exciting and entertaining, but they also showcase the best aspects of the sport – athleticism, strategy, and sportsmanship. Below we will we will explore some of the greatest games in football history.

Super Bowl III

Super Bowl III, played on January 12, 1969, is widely regarded as one of the greatest upsets in sports history. The New York Jets, led by quarterback Joe Namath, were heavy underdogs against the Baltimore Colts, who were considered one of the greatest teams of all time. However, Namath famously guaranteed a victory, and the Jets went on to win the game 16-7, with Namath being named the game's MVP.

Super Bowl XLII

Super Bowl XLII, played on February 3, 2008, was a matchup between the New England Patriots, who were attempting to complete an undefeated season, and the New York Giants. The Patriots were heavily favored, but the Giants defense put on a masterclass, sacking Patriots quarterback Tom Brady five times and holding the Patriots to just 14 points. The Giants pulled off the upset and won the game 17-14, with Eli Manning being named the game's MVP.

The 1958 NFL Championship Game

The 1958 NFL Championship Game, played on December 28, 1958, is often called "The Greatest Game Ever Played." The game was a back-and-forth affair between the Baltimore Colts and the New York Giants, with the lead changing hands several times. The game went into overtime, and Colts quarterback Johnny Unitas led his team on a game-winning drive, culminating in a touchdown pass to Alan Ameche. The game is credited with helping to popularize the NFL and turning it into the national pastime it is today.

The 1982 AFC Championship Game

The 1982 AFC Championship Game, played on January 10, 1983, was a matchup between the Miami Dolphins and the San Diego Chargers. The game was played in extremely cold and windy conditions, with wind chills dropping to -30 degrees. The game was a back-and-forth affair, with both teams trading blows throughout the game. The Chargers had a chance to win the game with a field goal in the final seconds, but the kick was blocked, and the game went into overtime. In overtime, Dolphins kicker Uwe von Schamann made a 34-yard field goal to win the game 41-38, in what is often called the "Epic in Miami."

The 2006 Rose Bowl

The 2006 Rose Bowl, played on January 4, 2006, was a matchup between the Texas Longhorns and the USC Trojans. The game was a battle between two Heisman Trophy-winning quarterbacks – USC's Matt Leinart and Texas' Vince Young. The game was a high-scoring affair, with both teams trading touchdowns throughout the game. In the final minutes, Vince Young led a game-winning drive, culminating in a touchdown run with just 19 seconds left on the clock. The game is often called one of the greatest college football games of all time.

Conclusion

The greatest games in football history are the ones that are still talked about years later, and they showcase the best aspects of the sport – athleticism, strategy, and sportsmanship. From the upsets of Super Bowl III and Super Bowl XLII, to the back-and-forth battles of the 1958 NFL Championship Game and the 1982 AFC Championship Game, to the high-scoring thriller of the 2006 Rose Bowl, these games are a testament

Memorable Super Bowls

The Super Bowl is the biggest annual sporting event in the United States, and has produced some of the most memorable moments in sports history. Every year, millions of people tune in to watch the game, and the Super Bowl has become more than just a football game – it's a cultural phenomenon. Below we will we will explore some of the most memorable Super Bowls in history.

Super Bowl III

Super Bowl III, played on January 12, 1969, is widely regarded as one of the greatest upsets in sports history. The New York Jets, led by quarterback Joe Namath, were heavy underdogs against the Baltimore Colts, who were considered one of the greatest teams of all time. However, Namath famously guaranteed a victory, and the Jets went on to win the game 16-7, with Namath being named the game's MVP. The victory helped legitimize the AFL, which merged with the NFL a few years later to form the modern NFL.

Super Bowl XXV

Super Bowl XXV, played on January 27, 1991, was a matchup between the Buffalo Bills and the New York Giants. The game is perhaps best remembered for the final drive by the Giants, which ate up over seven minutes of clock and ended with a game-winning field goal by kicker Matt Bahr. The Giants won the game 20-19, but the Bills' kicker Scott Norwood famously missed a potential game-winning field goal in the final seconds. The game was a defensive battle, with both teams struggling to move the ball, but it was ultimately decided by a single point.

Super Bowl XXXIV

Super Bowl XXXIV, played on January 30, 2000, was a matchup between the St. Louis Rams and the Tennessee Titans. The game is perhaps best remembered for the final play, which has been dubbed the "One Yard Short" play. With the Titans down by a touchdown in the final seconds of the game, quarterback Steve McNair led his team down the field and into the red zone. On the final play of the game, McNair completed a pass to receiver Kevin Dyson, who was tackled just short of the goal line. The Rams won the game 23-16, but the Titans' valiant effort in the final seconds is still remembered as one of the greatest finishes in Super Bowl history.

Super Bowl XLII

Super Bowl XLII, played on February 3, 2008, was a matchup between the New England Patriots, who were attempting to complete an undefeated season, and the New York Giants. The Patriots were heavily favored, but the Giants defense put on a masterclass, sacking Patriots quarterback Tom Brady five times and holding the Patriots to just 14 points. The Giants pulled off the upset and won the game 17-14, with Eli Manning being named the game's MVP. The game is often considered one of the greatest upsets in sports history, and it denied the Patriots their chance at a perfect season.

Super Bowl LI

Super Bowl LI, played on February 5, 2017, was a matchup between the New England Patriots and the Atlanta Falcons. The game was a back-and-forth affair, with the Falcons taking a commanding 28-3 lead in the third quarter. However, the Patriots mounted a comeback for the ages, scoring 25 unanswered points to tie the game and send it into overtime. In overtime, the Patriots won the coin toss and marched down the field to score the game-winning touchdown, winning the game 34-28. The game is often considered one of the greatest comebacks in sports history, and cemented the Patriots' legacy as one of the greatest dynasties in NFL history.

Classic college football games

College football is a sport steeped in tradition, and there have been countless classic games played over the years. These games have featured legendary players, iconic moments, and thrilling finishes that have left fans on the edge of their seats. Below we will we will explore some of the greatest classic college football games of all time.

1971 Nebraska vs. Oklahoma

On November 25, 1971, the No. 1 Nebraska Cornhuskers faced off against the No. 2 Oklahoma Sooners in a game that was dubbed the "Game of the Century." The two teams were both undefeated and were considered to be two of the greatest teams in college football history. The game lived up to the hype, with Nebraska winning 35-31 in a thrilling back-and-forth contest. The game is often considered one of the greatest in college football history, and it helped solidify Nebraska's place as a college football powerhouse.

1984 Boston College vs. Miami

On November 23, 1984, the Boston College Eagles faced off against the Miami Hurricanes in a game that would become known as the "Hail Flutie" game. With just seconds left on the clock, Boston College quarterback Doug Flutie launched a desperation pass that found its way into the hands of receiver Gerard Phelan, who scored the game-winning touchdown. The play, which has become known as the "Hail Mary" pass, is one of the most iconic moments in college football history, and it helped Flutie win the Heisman Trophy that year.

1. 2006 Rose Bowl: Texas vs. USC

On January 4, 2006, the Texas Longhorns faced off against the USC Trojans in the Rose Bowl, which was also the BCS National Championship game. The game featured two Heisman Trophy-winning quarterbacks in Vince Young and Matt Leinart, and it lived up to the hype. Young led the Longhorns on a game-winning drive in the final minutes of the game, capping it off with a touchdown run on fourth down with just 19 seconds left on the clock. The game is often considered one of the greatest college football games of all time, and it helped cement Young's legacy as one of the greatest college football players of all time.

2. 2007 Fiesta Bowl: Boise State vs. Oklahoma

On January 1, 2007, the Boise State Broncos faced off against the Oklahoma Sooners in the Fiesta Bowl. The game was a classic, with Boise State pulling off multiple trick plays and a game-tying touchdown in the final seconds of the game. The Broncos went on to win the game in overtime, capping off one of the most thrilling and improbable upsets in college football history. The game is often considered one of the greatest bowl games of all time, and it helped put Boise State on the map as a legitimate college football program.

3. 2013 Iron Bowl: Auburn vs. Alabama

On November 30, 2013, the Auburn Tigers faced off against the Alabama Crimson Tide in the Iron Bowl. The game featured two of the best teams in college football, and it lived up to the hype. With just seconds left on the clock, Alabama attempted a 57-yard field goal that fell short, and Auburn's Chris Davis caught the ball in the end zone and returned it 109 yards for the game-winning touchdown. The play, which has become known as the "Kick Six," is one of the most iconic moments in college football history, and it helped Auburn win the SEC Championship that year.

Rivalry games and upsets

Rivalry games and upsets are two of the most exciting aspects of college football. Rivalry games feature longstanding traditions, intense emotions, and often determine conference championships and bowl game eligibility. Upsets, on the other hand, see underdogs defeating heavily favored opponents, often causing chaos in the rankings and shaking up the college football landscape. Below we will we will explore some of the greatest rivalry games and upsets in college football history.

Rivalry Games

Ohio State vs. Michigan

The Ohio State Buckeyes and Michigan Wolverines have one of the most storied rivalries in all of sports. The two teams have been playing each other since 1897, and the annual matchup is known as "The Game." The rivalry is so intense that Ohio State head coach Woody Hayes famously refused to buy gas in the state of Michigan, and Michigan head coach Bo Schembechler once said, "I want to make sure that the people of Ohio are drinking soup with a fork."

Alabama vs. Auburn

The Iron Bowl is the annual matchup between the Alabama Crimson Tide and Auburn Tigers, two of the most successful programs in the SEC. The rivalry is named after the state's iron industry and has been played annually since 1948. The game has produced some memorable moments, including the "Kick Six" in 2013, which saw Auburn win the game on a 109-yard touchdown return of a missed field goal attempt.

Notre Dame vs. USC

The Notre Dame Fighting Irish and USC Trojans have a storied rivalry that dates back to 1926. The two teams have played each other over 90 times, and the rivalry is known for producing some of the most dramatic finishes in college football history. One of the most memorable moments in the rivalry came in 1974, when Notre Dame quarterback Tom Clements led the Fighting Irish on a game-winning drive in the final minutes of the game to secure a 55-24 victory.

Upsets

Appalachian State vs. Michigan

In 2007, the Appalachian State Mountaineers, a Division I-AA (now FCS) team, traveled to Ann Arbor to take on the Michigan Wolverines, who were ranked No. 5 in the nation. The Mountaineers shocked the world, winning the game 34-32 on a last-second field goal. It was the first time that a Division I-AA team had defeated a ranked Division I-A (now FBS) team, and it remains one of the greatest upsets in college football history.

Stanford vs. USC

In 2007, the Stanford Cardinal, a 41-point underdog, traveled to Los Angeles to take on the USC Trojans, who were ranked No. 1 in the nation. The game saw Stanford pull off one of the greatest upsets in college football history, winning the game 24-23 on a late field goal. The win was especially remarkable considering that Stanford had lost 41-3 to USC the previous year.

Boise State vs. Oklahoma

In the 2007 Fiesta Bowl, the Boise State Broncos, a mid-major program, faced off against the Oklahoma Sooners, who were ranked No. 7 in the nation. The game saw Boise State pull off one of the greatest upsets in college football history, winning the game 43-42 in overtime. The Broncos won the game on a trick play, with quarterback Jared Zabransky faking a pass and running for the game-winning touchdown.

The History and Evolution of the IFL

The Indoor Football League (IFL) is a professional indoor football league that was founded in 2008. The league has experienced significant growth and development over the years, with a strong emphasis on providing an exciting and entertaining game for fans. Below we will we will explore the history and evolution of the IFL.

History

1. The Indoor Football League was founded in 2008 by four former United Indoor Football teams: the Billings Outlaws, the Omaha Beef, the Sioux Falls Storm, and the Green Bay Blizzard. The league played its inaugural season in 2009 with six teams, including the founding four teams as well as the Fairbanks Grizzlies and the Alaska Wild. In the years that followed, the league expanded rapidly, with teams joining from all across the country.

Evolution

Rules and Gameplay

The IFL features a unique brand of indoor football that is designed to be fast-paced and exciting. The game is played on a field that is 50 yards long and 28 yards wide, which is much smaller than a traditional football field. The smaller field size allows for faster gameplay and more action-packed games. The IFL also features a number of other unique rules, such as the use of rebound nets on the end zone walls, which allows for the ball to stay in play longer and leads to more exciting plays.

Expansion and Contraction

Since its founding, the IFL has experienced both expansion and contraction. The league has added and lost teams over the years, as teams have come and gone based on a variety of factors such as financial stability and local interest. In recent years, the league has focused on expanding into new markets, with teams joining from all across the country.

Media Coverage

The IFL has also experienced growth in terms of media coverage over the years. The league has secured partnerships with a number of major media outlets, including ESPN and CBS Sports Network, which has helped to increase the visibility of the league and its teams. In addition, the league has embraced digital media, with games being streamed online and social media being used to promote the league and its teams.

Future Outlook

The future of the IFL is bright, with the league continuing to grow and develop. The league has added new teams in recent years, and there are plans to continue expanding into new markets. In addition, the league has continued to focus on providing an exciting and entertaining product for fans, which has helped to increase interest in the league.

Conclusion

The Indoor Football League has come a long way since its founding in 2008. The league has experienced significant growth and development over the years, with a strong emphasis on providing an exciting and entertaining game for fans. With new teams joining the league and a continued focus on expanding into new markets, the future of the IFL looks bright.

The Origins of Indoor Football

Indoor football is a unique and exciting variation of American football that is played in a smaller indoor arena. It is a sport that has grown in popularity over the years, with professional and amateur leagues across the country. Below we will we will explore the origins of indoor football and how it has evolved over time.

The history of indoor football dates back to the 1930s when a number of organizations began experimenting with different variations of the game. The first recorded indoor football game was played on December 29, 1932, between two high school teams in Chicago, Illinois. The game was played in the Chicago Stadium, which had a seating capacity of 17,000 people.

The popularity of indoor football grew in the 1960s and 1970s, with a number of leagues and teams forming across the country. One of the most successful indoor football leagues of this era was the Continental Football League, which played from 1965 to 1969. The league featured a number of successful teams, including the Florida Blazers and the Charleston Rockets.

In the 1980s, indoor football experienced a resurgence in popularity, with the formation of the Arena Football League (AFL) in 1987. The AFL was founded by Jim Foster, a former NFL executive, who saw the potential for a fast-paced and high-scoring version of football that could be played indoors. The AFL featured a number of unique rules, such as the use of rebound nets on the end zone walls, which allowed for more exciting plays and a faster pace of gameplay.

The AFL quickly became popular with fans, and the league expanded rapidly over the years, with teams joining from all across the country. The league also attracted a number of high-profile players, including Kurt Warner, who went on to have a successful career in the NFL after playing for the Iowa Barnstormers in the AFL.

In addition to the AFL, a number of other indoor football leagues formed in the 1980s and 1990s, including the World Indoor Football League and the Professional Indoor Football League. These leagues featured a variety of unique rules and gameplay styles, and many of them enjoyed success for a number of years.

In recent years, indoor football has continued to grow in popularity, with new leagues and teams forming across the country. One of the most successful of these new leagues is the Indoor Football League (IFL), which was founded in 2008. The IFL features a unique brand of indoor football that is designed to be fast-paced and exciting, with a number of unique rules and gameplay features.

Today, indoor football is played at both the amateur and professional levels, with leagues and teams across the country. The sport continues to evolve and develop, with new rules and gameplay features being added to make the game even more exciting for fans.

In conclusion, indoor football is a unique and exciting variation of American football that has a rich history dating back to the 1930s. The sport has evolved over time, with a number of different leagues and rules being developed to make the game more exciting for fans. Today, indoor football continues to grow in popularity, with new leagues and teams forming across the country. With its fast-paced gameplay and high-scoring action, indoor football is sure to remain a popular sport for years to come.

The Formation of the IFL

The Indoor Football League (IFL) is one of the premier indoor football leagues in the United States, featuring a unique brand of fast-paced and high-scoring football that has captivated fans across the country. Below we will we will explore the formation of the IFL and how it has evolved over time.

The IFL was founded in 2008 by a group of investors led by John Morris, the owner of the Spokane Shock, a successful indoor football team based in Spokane, Washington. The league was formed with the goal of creating a more stable and financially viable model for indoor football, which had been plagued by a number of problems in previous years.

One of the key factors in the formation of the IFL was the decision to adopt a single-entity ownership structure, which meant that all of the teams in the league were owned by the league itself, rather than individual owners. This allowed the league to maintain greater control over its operations and finances, and also helped to reduce the risk of teams folding or leaving the league.

Another important aspect of the IFL's formation was the decision to focus on a small number of high-quality teams, rather than trying to grow too quickly and risking the quality of the product. The league initially started with just six teams, but has since grown to include more than a dozen teams from across the country.

One of the unique features of the IFL is its focus on developing young players and helping them to advance to higher levels of football. The league has established partnerships with a number of college football programs, allowing players to continue their development while also getting exposure to professional teams.

Over the years, the IFL has continued to evolve and develop, with new rules and gameplay features being introduced to make the game even more exciting for fans. One of the most significant changes in recent years has been the adoption of a franchise model, which allows individual owners to purchase and operate their own teams within the league.

The IFL has also been successful in attracting a number of high-profile players and coaches over the years, including former NFL players and coaches. This has helped to raise the profile of the league and attract even more fans to the sport.

In addition to its focus on high-quality football, the IFL is also committed to giving back to the communities in which it operates. The league has established a number of programs and initiatives to support local charities and organizations, and many of its teams are actively involved in community outreach and volunteer work.

In conclusion, the formation of the IFL was a significant milestone in the development of indoor football in the United States. The league's unique ownership structure, focus on quality over quantity, and commitment to player development and community outreach have helped to make it one of the most successful and popular indoor football leagues in the country. With its fast-paced and exciting style of play, the IFL is sure to continue to captivate fans for years to come.

Key Figures in the Development of the League

The development and success of any sports league is heavily influenced by the key figures who help to shape and guide it. The Indoor Football League (IFL) is no exception, and Below we will we will examine some of the key figures who have played a significant role in the development and growth of the league.

John Morris - Founder of the IFL

John Morris is the founder of the IFL and the owner of the Spokane Shock, one of the league's most successful franchises. Morris was instrumental in the formation of the league and played a key role in establishing its single-entity ownership structure, which has helped to ensure the stability and financial viability of the league.

Tommy Benizio - Former Commissioner of the IFL

Tommy Benizio served as the Commissioner of the IFL from 2011 to 2014 and played a significant role in shaping the league during his tenure. Benizio helped to expand the league's reach by bringing in new teams and creating partnerships with other organizations, and also introduced a number of new rules and gameplay features to make the game more exciting for fans.

Robert Loving - Former IFL Team Owner

Robert Loving was the owner of the Bloomington Edge, one of the IFL's most successful franchises, from 2010 to 2019. Loving was a key figure in the league's expansion and helped to establish the IFL as one of the premier indoor football leagues in the country. He was also known for his commitment to community outreach and philanthropy, which helped to raise the profile of the league and its teams.

Adam Nebeker - IFL Executive Director

Adam Nebeker currently serves as the Executive Director of the IFL and has played a significant role in the league's recent growth and success. Nebeker has helped to streamline the league's operations and finances, and has worked to create new opportunities for player development and community outreach.

Kurt Warner - Former IFL Player

Kurt Warner is a former NFL quarterback who got his start in professional football playing for the Iowa Barnstormers in the Arena Football League, a precursor to the IFL. Warner's success in the AFL helped to raise the profile of indoor football and played a significant role in attracting new fans and players to the sport.

Dixie Wooten - Current Head Coach of the Iowa Barnstormers

Dixie Wooten is the current head coach of the Iowa Barnstormers and has led the team to multiple playoff appearances and a championship title. Wooten is known for his innovative coaching strategies and his ability to develop young players, and has become one of the most respected coaches in the league.

Bernie Connelly - IFL Hall of Fame Inductee

Bernie Connelly is a former player and coach in the IFL and was inducted into the league's Hall of Fame in 2016. Connelly played a significant role in the development of the IFL's rules and gameplay features, and was known for his commitment to fair play and sportsmanship.

In conclusion, the success of the Indoor Football League can be attributed to the contributions of a number of key figures who have helped to shape and guide the league over the years. From its founder John Morris to its current Executive Director Adam Nebeker, the IFL has been fortunate to have the guidance of passionate and committed individuals who have helped to establish the league as one of the premier indoor football organizations in the country.

The Growth and Expansion of the IFL

The Indoor Football League (IFL) has experienced significant growth and expansion since its founding in 2008. The league has added new teams and expanded into new markets, attracting more fans and players to the sport of indoor football. Below we will we will examine the factors that have contributed to the growth and expansion of the IFL.

Single-Entity Ownership

The IFL's single-entity ownership structure, in which all teams are owned and operated by the league itself, has helped to ensure the stability and financial viability of the league. This model allows for more centralized control over the league's finances, marketing, and other operations, and has helped to prevent the kind of financial struggles that have plagued other professional sports leagues.

Expansion into New Markets

One of the key drivers of the IFL's growth has been the league's expansion into new markets. Since its founding, the IFL has added new teams in cities such as Cedar Rapids, Iowa; Sioux Falls, South Dakota; and Bismarck, North Dakota. This expansion has helped to broaden the league's geographic reach and attract new fans to the sport.

Innovative Rule Changes

The IFL has introduced a number of innovative rule changes and gameplay features that have made the game more exciting for fans and players. For example, the league has adopted a 50-yard field, which allows for a faster-paced game and more scoring opportunities. The IFL has also implemented a "one-platoon" system, in which players play both offense and defense, adding an additional layer of strategy to the game.

Strong Community Involvement

The IFL has placed a strong emphasis on community involvement and outreach, which has helped to raise the profile of the league and its teams. Many IFL teams are actively involved in local charities and community organizations, and the league has also partnered with other organizations to promote youth football and other community initiatives.

High-Quality Play and Player Development

The IFL has attracted a number of high-quality players, including former NFL and college stars, who have helped to raise the level of play in the league. The IFL has also implemented a number of player development programs, such as the IFL Player Combine and the IFL/NFL Regional Combine, which provide opportunities for players to showcase their skills and potentially move on to higher levels of play.

Commitment to Fan Experience

The IFL has made a concerted effort to enhance the fan experience, both in-person and through digital channels. The league has implemented fan-friendly policies such as low ticket prices, free parking, and post-game player meet-and-greets, and has also invested in digital platforms to provide fans with access to live games, highlights, and other content.

Partnership with Other Leagues

The IFL has established partnerships with other indoor football leagues, such as Champions Indoor Football (CIF) and the National Arena League (NAL), which has helped to create a more unified and competitive indoor football landscape. These partnerships have also provided opportunities for cross-promotion and increased exposure for the IFL and its teams.

In conclusion, the growth and expansion of the Indoor Football League can be attributed to a combination of factors, including innovative rule changes, strong community involvement, high-quality play and player development, and a commitment to fan experience. The league's single-entity ownership structure and partnerships with other leagues have also helped to ensure its financial stability and competitiveness. As the league continues to expand into new markets and attract new fans and players, the future of the IFL looks bright.

Football and American Culture

Football has become a staple of American culture, deeply ingrained in the country's identity and values. From the fervent support of local high school teams to the spectacle of the Super Bowl, football has woven itself into the fabric of American society. Below we will we will examine the ways in which football has become a cultural phenomenon in the United States.

Community and Identity

Football has long been a way for communities to come together and rally around a common cause. High school and college football games are often the centerpieces of small towns and universities, bringing together students, families, and local residents. The shared experience of rooting for a team can create a sense of identity and belonging, and football has become a way for many Americans to connect with their communities.

Values and Traditions

Football also embodies many of the values and traditions that are important to American culture. The emphasis on hard work, discipline, and teamwork that is inherent in football mirrors the values that are prized in American society. Additionally, football has its own set of traditions, from tailgating and game-day rituals to the iconic Thanksgiving Day games. These traditions have become a part of American culture, and are eagerly anticipated by fans every year.

National Pride

Football has become a source of national pride for many Americans, particularly when it comes to the NFL. The Super Bowl has become a cultural event in its own right, with millions of viewers tuning in to watch the game each year. The pageantry and spectacle of the Super Bowl halftime show, combined with the game itself, have made it one of the most-watched events on television. Additionally, the NFL has become a way for Americans to demonstrate their patriotism and love of country, with military tributes and displays of the American flag at games.

Economic Impact

Football also has a significant economic impact on American culture. The NFL alone generates billions of dollars in revenue each year, and has created countless jobs in industries such as broadcasting, advertising, and hospitality. Additionally, high school and college football programs contribute to local economies, with fans and visitors coming to town to attend games and support their teams.

Social Issues

Football has also become intertwined with social issues in American culture. The NFL has been at the center of debates around issues such as player protests during the national anthem and the long-term health effects of concussions. Additionally, football has been used as a platform to raise awareness for social causes, such as breast cancer and racial injustice. These conversations have become a part of the national dialogue, and have sparked important discussions about the role of sports in society.

In conclusion, football has become a cultural phenomenon in the United States, with a deep and lasting impact on American society. From its ability to bring communities together to its embodiment of American values and traditions, football has become a way for Americans to connect with each other and with their country. As the sport continues to evolve and face new challenges, its place in American culture will undoubtedly continue to be a topic of fascination and debate.

Impact on society

Football, both college and professional, has had a significant impact on society in the United States. From shaping popular culture to influencing social issues, football has become an integral part of American society. Below we will we will explore the various ways in which football has impacted American society.

Pop Culture

Football has had a tremendous impact on popular culture in the United States. From movies and television shows to video games, football has become a staple of entertainment. The Super Bowl halftime show, for example, has become a cultural event in its own right, with performers such as Beyoncé and Lady Gaga putting on memorable performances. Additionally, football-themed movies and TV shows, such as Friday Night Lights and Remember the Titans, have become classics in American popular culture.

Economic Impact

Football has also had a significant economic impact on society. The NFL alone generates billions of dollars in revenue each year, with the Super Bowl being one of the most-watched events on television. Additionally, high school and college football programs contribute to local economies, with fans and visitors coming to town to attend games and support their teams. The economic impact of football extends beyond just the sport itself, with industries such as advertising and hospitality benefiting from the popularity of football.

Social Issues

Football has become intertwined with social issues in American society. The NFL has been at the center of debates around issues such as player protests during the national anthem and the long-term health effects of concussions. Additionally, football has been used as a platform to raise awareness for social causes, such as breast cancer and racial injustice. These conversations have become a part of the national dialogue, and have sparked important discussions about the role of sports in society.

Education

Football has also had an impact on education in the United States. College football, in particular, has become a way for universities to showcase their schools and attract students. The success of a college football program can have a significant impact on enrollment, and universities often invest heavily in their football programs to attract top talent. Additionally, high school football programs can provide opportunities for students to develop leadership skills and learn the importance of teamwork.

Community and Identity

Football has long been a way for communities to come together and rally around a common cause. High school and college football games are often the centerpieces of small towns and universities, bringing together students, families, and local residents. The shared experience of rooting for a team can create a sense of identity and belonging, and football has become a way for many Americans to connect with their communities.

In conclusion, football has had a significant impact on society in the United States. From shaping popular culture to influencing social issues, football has become an integral part of American society. As the sport continues to evolve and face new challenges, its impact on society will undoubtedly continue to be a topic of fascination and debate.

Movies, books, and music

Movies, books, and music have all been influenced by football in various ways. From inspiring sports films to providing a backdrop for musical performances, football has become a recurring theme in popular culture. Below we will we will explore the ways in which football has influenced movies, books, and music.

Movies

Football has been the inspiration for many popular movies over the years. From biopics about legendary coaches and players to fictional stories about high school and college football, there are numerous films that have been made about football. Some of the most iconic football movies include Rudy, Remember the Titans, The Blind Side, and Friday Night Lights. These movies not only entertain viewers but also inspire them with stories of perseverance, teamwork, and triumph.

Books

Football has also been the subject of many books, both fiction and nonfiction. Biographies of legendary players and coaches, such as Walter Payton and Vince Lombardi, have become bestsellers. Nonfiction books about the inner workings of the NFL, such as Friday Night Lights author Buzz Bissinger's Three Nights in August, provide readers with a behind-the-scenes look at the world of professional football. Additionally, fictional works such as Friday Night Lights, The Art of Fielding, and The Last Boy offer unique perspectives on the sport.

Music

Football has also had an impact on the music industry. Many artists have written songs about football, from Johnny Cash's "The Man in Black" to Hank Williams Jr.'s "All My Rowdy Friends Are Coming Over Tonight." Additionally, football has been the backdrop for many musical performances, such as Lady Gaga's iconic halftime show at the 2017 Super Bowl. The marching bands that perform at high school and college football games are also an important part of the musical aspect of football.

Inspiration

Football has inspired many artists across different mediums. The dedication, discipline, and teamwork required to succeed in football are values that many artists find compelling. Additionally, the personal stories of players and coaches, as well as the larger cultural impact of football, have been the inspiration for many creative works. Football has become a way for artists to explore themes of identity, community, and resilience.

In conclusion, football has had a significant impact on popular culture, inspiring artists across different mediums to create works that explore the sport's unique themes and stories. From movies and books to music, football has become an integral part of American culture. As the sport continues to evolve and inspire, it is likely that we will see even more works of art inspired by football in the future.

The role of fandom

Football fandom has become a cultural phenomenon that transcends the sport itself. Fans of football, commonly known as "fanatics," have a deep emotional connection to the sport and their favorite teams, players, and coaches. Below we will we will explore the role of fandom in football and its impact on the sport.

Emotional Connection

Football fandom is rooted in the emotional connection that fans feel towards their favorite teams. Fans often describe their fandom as a part of their identity, and they invest a significant amount of time, energy, and money in supporting their team. The emotional connection to the sport is often passed down through generations, with parents passing on their love for a particular team to their children. Fans feel a sense of belonging to a larger community of supporters, and this shared emotional connection creates a sense of camaraderie and unity.

Impact on the Sport

The role of fandom in football extends beyond the emotional connection that fans have to the sport. Fans also have a significant impact on the sport itself, from influencing team decisions to shaping the culture of football. Fan support is critical to the success of a team, as it provides the financial resources necessary to fund the team's operations. Additionally, fan feedback is often taken into consideration when teams make decisions about players, coaches, and even the design of team uniforms.

Fan Culture

Football fandom has also given rise to a unique fan culture that includes traditions, rituals, and even a language of its own. Fans create elaborate tailgating experiences before games, wear team colors and merchandise, and participate in chants and cheers during games. Fan culture has become a part of the larger football culture, with traditions such as the "Lambeau Leap" at Green Bay Packers games and the "Hail Mary" play being recognized across the sport.

Technology and Social Media

The role of fandom in football has been transformed by technology and social media. Fans can now connect with each other and their favorite teams and players through social media platforms such as Twitter, Instagram, and Facebook. This has allowed fans to engage with the sport on a deeper level, and has created new opportunities for teams and players to connect with their fans.

In conclusion, football fandom plays a significant role in the sport, from the emotional connection that fans have to the impact they have on the sport itself. Fan culture has become an integral part of the larger football culture, and technology has transformed the way fans engage with the sport. As football continues to evolve, it is likely that fandom will continue to play a vital role in the sport's growth and success.

The Business of Football

Football is a multi-billion dollar industry that generates enormous revenues for teams, leagues, and other stakeholders. Below we will we will explore the business of football and its impact on the sport.

Revenue Streams

The primary revenue streams for football include broadcasting rights, sponsorships, merchandise sales, and ticket sales. Broadcasting rights are among the most significant revenue streams, with broadcasters paying billions of dollars to secure the rights to air games. Sponsorships from companies such as Nike and Coca-Cola also provide a significant source of revenue, with teams and leagues receiving millions of dollars in exchange for displaying sponsor logos on their uniforms and in their stadiums. Merchandise sales, including jerseys, hats, and other team-branded items, generate billions of dollars in revenue each year. Finally, ticket sales for games provide teams and leagues with another significant source of revenue.

Team Valuations

The value of football teams has skyrocketed in recent years, with many of the world's top teams now worth billions of dollars. According to Forbes, the most valuable football team in the world is the Dallas Cowboys, valued at $6.5 billion. Other teams in the top ten include Manchester United, Real Madrid, and Barcelona. The high value of football teams has been driven in part by the increasing revenues generated by the sport, as well as the global popularity of football.

Salary Structures

Football players are among the highest-paid athletes in the world, with top players earning millions of dollars per year. The salary structures for football players vary depending on the league, team, and player. In the NFL, for example, players earn a base salary plus bonuses, and contracts often include clauses related to performance and playing time. In European football leagues, players often receive a base salary plus performance bonuses and appearance fees. The highest-paid football player in the world is currently Lionel Messi, who earns more than $130 million per year.

Impact on Local Economies

Football can have a significant impact on local economies, particularly in cities where teams are based. The presence of a football team can create jobs, increase tourism, and generate revenue for local businesses such as hotels, restaurants, and bars. Additionally, the construction of new stadiums or renovations to existing ones can create jobs and stimulate economic growth. However, some critics argue that the economic impact of football on local economies is often overstated and that the costs associated with building new stadiums or hosting major events such as the Super Bowl often outweigh the economic benefits.

Social Responsibility

As football has become increasingly lucrative, teams and leagues have faced increased pressure to act responsibly and give back to their communities. Many teams and leagues now have programs focused on social responsibility, such as initiatives aimed at reducing their carbon footprint, supporting local charities, and promoting diversity and inclusion. Additionally, some leagues and teams have implemented programs focused on player safety, such as concussion protocols and rules aimed at reducing the risk of head injuries.

In conclusion, the business of football has become a major industry that generates enormous revenues for teams, leagues, and other stakeholders. The value of football teams has skyrocketed in recent years, and football players are among the highest-paid athletes in the world. While football can have a significant impact on local economies, it is also important for teams and leagues to act responsibly and give back to their communities. As football continues to grow and evolve, it is likely that the business of football will continue to play a significant role in the sport's future.

Team ownership and management

The ownership and management of football teams are critical components of the sport. Owners and managers play a vital role in shaping the success of a team, from hiring coaches and players to developing a winning strategy. Below we will we will explore the role of team ownership and management in football.

Team Ownership

Team ownership in football can take many different forms, from individual owners to corporate entities. In many cases, team ownership is a significant investment, with owners spending millions of dollars to purchase a team. Some team owners are also involved in other industries, using their experience and resources to build successful football franchises.

Responsibilities of Team Owners

The primary responsibility of team owners is to ensure that their team is successful both on and off the field. This involves investing in the team's infrastructure, such as stadiums and training facilities, and hiring qualified staff to manage the team's operations. Team owners are also responsible for making critical decisions related to player personnel, such as hiring and firing coaches and signing players.

Team Management

Team management involves overseeing the day-to-day operations of a football team, from managing player contracts to scheduling games and practices. Management teams may include general managers, coaches, and other staff who work together to develop a winning strategy and execute it on the field. In many cases, team management is responsible for developing long-term plans for the team, such as rebuilding efforts or developing new talent pipelines.

Building a Winning Team

One of the primary responsibilities of team ownership and management is to build a winning team. This involves identifying and acquiring talented players who can perform well on the field and help the team achieve its goals. Building a winning team also requires a strong coaching staff that can develop effective game strategies and train players to perform at their best.

Managing Team Finances

Another critical responsibility of team ownership and management is managing team finances. This includes developing and managing team budgets, negotiating contracts with players and staff, and ensuring that the team is operating within its financial means. Effective financial management is critical for ensuring that the team can remain competitive over the long term.

Balancing the Business and Sport of Football

The ownership and management of football teams must balance the business and sport of football. While the ultimate goal of any team is to win games and championships, team owners and management must also consider the financial implications of their decisions. This may involve making difficult decisions related to player personnel or investing in team infrastructure to enhance the team's revenue streams.

In conclusion, team ownership and management are critical components of the sport of football. Team owners and management teams must work together to build successful teams, develop winning strategies, and manage team finances. Balancing the business and sport of football can be challenging, but effective team ownership and management can help ensure that a team remains competitive over the long term.

Stadiums and facilities

Stadiums and facilities play a crucial role in the world of football. They are not only essential for hosting games and accommodating fans but also for providing athletes with a space to train and develop their skills. Below we will we will explore the significance of stadiums and facilities in football.

Stadiums

Stadiums are purpose-built facilities that are designed to host football games. They provide a space for fans to come together to support their favorite teams and for athletes to showcase their skills on the field. Modern stadiums are equipped with state-of-the-art technology, such as giant video screens and sound systems, that enhance the fan experience.

Types of Stadiums

There are several types of stadiums used in football, including indoor and outdoor facilities. Outdoor stadiums are the most common and are often designed with natural grass fields. Indoor stadiums, on the other hand, are climate-controlled and often have artificial turf fields. These facilities are ideal for hosting games in extreme weather conditions, and they also offer a more controlled environment for television broadcasts.

Stadium Design

Stadium design has evolved significantly over the years, with modern stadiums incorporating cutting-edge technology and amenities. Many stadiums feature retractable roofs and walls, allowing them to be used in a variety of weather conditions. They also include various seating arrangements, from luxury boxes to general admission sections, to accommodate fans of all types.

Fan Experience

Stadiums play a significant role in providing fans with an immersive and enjoyable experience. Modern stadiums offer a range of amenities, such as concession stands, team stores, and fan zones, where fans can engage with other fans and experience the excitement of the game. Additionally, stadiums often feature in-game entertainment, such as live music and halftime shows, to keep fans engaged throughout the game.

Training Facilities

In addition to stadiums, training facilities are an essential component of football. These facilities provide athletes with a space to develop their skills and prepare for games. Training facilities often include state-of-the-art equipment and technology, such as virtual reality training systems and performance tracking software.

Types of Training Facilities

There are several types of training facilities used in football, including team training facilities and player development centers. Team training facilities are used by entire teams to practice and prepare for games, while player development centers are used by individual players to work on their skills and improve their performance.

Facility Design

Like stadiums, the design of training facilities has evolved significantly over the years. Modern facilities often include a range of amenities, such as weight rooms, cardio equipment, and specialized training areas for specific positions. They also incorporate cutting-edge technology, such as motion tracking systems and advanced analytics software, to help athletes improve their performance.

Importance of Facilities

Stadiums and training facilities are critical components of the football industry. They not only provide a space for athletes to train and compete but also create jobs and generate revenue for communities. Additionally, state-of-the-art facilities can attract top talent and help teams remain competitive over the long term.

In conclusion, stadiums and facilities are essential components of the football industry. They provide a space for athletes to train and compete, create an immersive fan experience, and generate revenue for communities. As the industry continues to evolve, the design and technology used in stadiums and training facilities will continue to play a critical role in the success of football teams.

Sponsorships and endorsements

Sponsorships and endorsements have become an integral part of the football industry. They provide teams and individual players with the opportunity to generate revenue and increase their visibility, while also allowing companies to reach their target audience through association with the sport. Below we will we will explore the significance of sponsorships and endorsements in football.

Sponsorships

Sponsorships are agreements between companies and teams or leagues that provide financial support in exchange for branding and promotional opportunities. These agreements can include a range of benefits, such as stadium naming rights, jersey sponsorships, and in-game advertising. Sponsors can also provide teams with products and services, such as equipment and transportation, which can help reduce operating costs.

Endorsements

Endorsements are agreements between companies and individual players that allow the company to use the player's name, image, and likeness for promotional purposes. These agreements can include a range of benefits, such as advertising campaigns, product endorsements, and personal appearances. Endorsements can provide players with significant financial rewards, while also increasing their exposure and marketability.

Benefits of Sponsorships and Endorsements

Sponsorships and endorsements provide numerous benefits to both teams and players. They can generate significant revenue, which can be used to invest in infrastructure, hire top talent, and provide fans with a better experience. Additionally, they can increase the visibility and marketability of both teams and players, making them more attractive to fans and potential sponsors.

Impact on Fans

Sponsorships and endorsements can also have a significant impact on fans. They can provide fans with access to new products and services, such as team-branded merchandise and special promotions. Additionally, they can help enhance the overall fan experience by providing additional entertainment and engagement opportunities.

Challenges of Sponsorships and Endorsements

While sponsorships and endorsements offer numerous benefits, they also present several challenges. For teams, managing multiple sponsorships can be complex and time-consuming, and negotiating fair terms can be challenging. For players, managing their personal brand can be challenging, and navigating potential conflicts of interest can be difficult.

Ethics and Regulations

Sponsorships and endorsements have come under increased scrutiny in recent years, with concerns around ethics and regulations. For example, there have been concerns around the influence of sponsorships on team and league decisions, as well as concerns around the use of performance-enhancing products by athletes. As a result, regulatory bodies have put in place guidelines and regulations to ensure that sponsorships and endorsements are ethical and fair.

Future of Sponsorships and Endorsements

As the football industry continues to evolve, sponsorships and endorsements are likely to become even more important. The rise of social media and digital platforms has created new opportunities for companies to reach fans and athletes, and the use of data and analytics is helping companies to better target their audiences. Additionally, the growth of e-sports and virtual reality is creating new opportunities for sponsorships and endorsements in the gaming industry.

In conclusion, sponsorships and endorsements have become a critical component of the football industry. They provide teams and individual players with the opportunity to generate revenue and increase their visibility, while also allowing companies to reach their target audience through association with the sport. While there are challenges and ethical considerations associated with sponsorships and endorsements, their importance is likely to continue to grow in the future as the industry continues to evolve.

Fantasy Football

Fantasy football has become a popular pastime for millions of fans around the world. It involves selecting a virtual team of real-life players and competing against other fantasy teams based on the actual performance of those players in real-life games. Below we will we will explore the significance of fantasy football, its history, and the impact it has had on the football industry.

Origins of Fantasy Football

The origins of fantasy football can be traced back to the 1960s, when a group of sports journalists created a fantasy baseball league. The concept was later adapted for football, and the first fantasy football league was reportedly started in 1969. The game gained popularity throughout the 1980s and 1990s, and the rise of the internet in the 2000s led to an explosion in popularity.

How Fantasy Football Works

In fantasy football, participants typically form a league and draft a team of players from real-life NFL teams. Each week, the fantasy team competes against another team in the league, with points awarded based on the performance of the players in the real-life games. Points can be awarded for touchdowns, yards gained, and other statistical categories. The team with the most points at the end of the season is declared the winner.

Significance of Fantasy Football

Fantasy football has become a significant part of the football industry. It has helped increase the popularity of the sport and has given fans a new way to engage with the game. Fantasy football has also generated significant revenue for the NFL, with companies paying for the rights to use NFL logos and player images in their fantasy games.

Impact on Fan Engagement

Fantasy football has had a significant impact on fan engagement. It has given fans a vested interest in the performance of individual players and teams, which can lead to increased viewership and interest in the sport. It has also given fans a new way to interact with each other and has created a sense of community among fans.

Impact on the NFL

Fantasy football has also had a significant impact on the NFL. It has increased the overall popularity of the sport, which has led to increased revenue from ticket sales, merchandise, and broadcasting rights. Additionally, the game has helped the NFL reach new audiences, particularly younger fans who may not have been interested in the sport otherwise.

Challenges of Fantasy Football

Despite its popularity, fantasy football is not without its challenges. The game can be time-consuming, with participants spending hours researching players, analyzing statistics, and making lineup decisions. Additionally, the game can sometimes detract from the actual on-field action, with fans more interested in the performance of their fantasy team than the actual outcome of the game.

Future of Fantasy Football

As the football industry continues to evolve, fantasy football is likely to remain an important part of the sport. The rise of new technologies, such as virtual reality and augmented reality, may lead to new forms of fantasy football that are even more immersive and engaging. Additionally, the game is likely to continue to evolve, with new scoring systems and rules introduced to keep the game fresh and engaging for fans.

In conclusion, fantasy football has become a significant part of the football industry. It has helped increase the popularity of the sport and has given fans a new way to engage with the game. Fantasy football has also generated significant revenue for the NFL and has helped the league reach new audiences. While the game is not without its challenges, its importance is likely to continue to grow in the future as the industry continues to evolve.

Draft strategies and player rankings

The NFL draft is an exciting time for football fans, as teams work to build their rosters for the upcoming season. Draft strategies and player rankings play a crucial role in determining which teams are successful in building a winning team. Below we will we will explore the significance of draft strategies and player rankings and how they can impact a team's success.

Importance of Draft Strategies

Draft strategies are essential for a team's success in building a competitive roster. Teams must carefully analyze their strengths and weaknesses to determine which players will fit into their system and address areas of need. This can involve targeting players who possess specific skills or attributes that are necessary for success in certain positions or schemes.

Key Factors in Draft Strategies

Several key factors can impact a team's draft strategy. These include the team's current roster makeup, the availability of players at certain positions, the depth of talent in the draft class, and the team's overall draft position. Teams must also consider the long-term implications of their draft choices, as drafting the wrong player can set the team back for years to come.

Player Rankings

Player rankings play a crucial role in draft strategies, as they provide teams with a guide for which players are the most valuable and should be targeted in the draft. Rankings are typically based on a player's overall talent level, production in college, and potential for success at the next level. These rankings can vary widely among different draft experts and media outlets, and teams must carefully evaluate the players on their own to make the best decisions.

Importance of Scouting

Scouting is a critical aspect of drafting, as teams must evaluate players based on more than just their statistics and rankings. Teams must take into account a player's intangibles, such as work ethic, leadership, and football IQ, to determine how they will fit into the team's culture and system. Scouting can also involve evaluating a player's character and off-field behavior to ensure they are a good fit for the team.

Draft Strategies in Action

Effective draft strategies can be seen in action in the success of teams like the New England Patriots, who have consistently built winning rosters through smart draft picks and strategic player acquisitions. The Patriots have been known for their focus on character and football IQ, as well as their ability to identify talent in later rounds of the draft.

Common Draft Strategies

Some common draft strategies include targeting players at positions of need, taking the best player available regardless of position, and trading up or down in the draft to acquire the right players. Teams may also focus on building through the draft or supplementing their roster through free agency and trades.

Future of Draft Strategies and Player Rankings

As the football industry continues to evolve, draft strategies and player rankings are likely to become even more important. The rise of new technologies, such as advanced analytics and machine learning, may lead to new approaches to player evaluation and draft strategy. Additionally, changes in the game itself, such as the increasing emphasis on speed and agility, may impact which attributes teams prioritize in their draft choices.

In conclusion, draft strategies and player rankings play a crucial role in a team's success in building a competitive roster. Teams must carefully analyze their strengths and weaknesses, scout players thoroughly, and make smart draft choices to build a winning team. As the football industry continues to evolve, draft strategies and player rankings are likely to become even more critical, as teams seek to gain an edge in a highly competitive landscape.

Managing your team

Managing a football team is no easy task. It requires a combination of leadership, communication, strategic thinking, and a deep understanding of the game. Below we will we will explore the key principles and strategies for effectively managing a football team.

Building a Strong Team Culture

The foundation of any successful team is a strong team culture. This involves creating a shared set of values, goals, and expectations that guide the behavior and interactions of everyone on the team. A strong team culture helps to foster trust, accountability, and a sense of belonging among team members.

Effective Communication

Effective communication is essential for successful team management. This involves not only communicating the team's goals and expectations but also providing regular feedback to individual players to help them improve. It also involves creating an open and transparent environment where players feel comfortable sharing their ideas and concerns.

Setting Goals and Objectives

Setting clear goals and objectives is essential for keeping the team focused and motivated. This can involve setting both short-term and long-term goals, such as winning a particular game, winning a championship, or developing specific skills or abilities. Goals should be realistic, measurable, and achievable, and progress towards them should be regularly monitored and evaluated.

Creating and Implementing Game Plans

Game planning is a critical aspect of football management. This involves analyzing the opponent's strengths and weaknesses, identifying key matchups, and developing a strategy for success. Effective game planning requires a deep understanding of the game and the ability to make quick decisions and adjustments based on changing circumstances.

Managing Player Performance and Development

Managing player performance and development is a critical aspect of football management. This involves setting expectations for each player's role on the team, providing regular feedback and support, and creating opportunities for player development and improvement. Effective player management requires a deep understanding of each player's strengths and weaknesses and the ability to create a personalized development plan for each player.

Building and Managing Relationships

Building and managing relationships is a critical aspect of football management. This involves developing relationships with players, coaching staff, and other key stakeholders, such as team owners, sponsors, and media representatives. Effective relationship management requires strong communication skills, empathy, and a willingness to listen to and understand others' perspectives.

Managing Resources

Managing resources is a critical aspect of football management. This involves managing the team's budget, facilities, equipment, and other resources to ensure that the team has the necessary resources to succeed. Effective resource management requires a deep understanding of the team's needs and priorities and the ability to make strategic decisions that balance short-term and long-term goals.

In conclusion, effective team management requires a combination of leadership, communication, strategic thinking, and a deep understanding of the game. By building a strong team culture, communicating effectively, setting goals and objectives, creating and implementing game plans, managing player performance and development, building and managing relationships, and managing resources, football managers can create a winning team and a culture of success.

The growth of daily fantasy sports

Daily fantasy sports (DFS) have exploded in popularity over the past decade, with millions of people around the world participating in daily and weekly contests for cash prizes. Below we will we will explore the growth of daily fantasy sports and the key factors driving this trend.

Technological Advances

One of the primary drivers of the growth of daily fantasy sports has been technological advances. The rise of mobile devices, high-speed internet connections, and data analytics has enabled DFS operators to offer a seamless and immersive user experience that was not possible just a few years ago. Today, users can easily create and manage their lineups, track live scores and updates, and make real-time changes to their roster using just their mobile device.

Increased Legalization and Regulation

Another key factor driving the growth of daily fantasy sports is the increased legalization and regulation of the industry. In the past, daily fantasy sports was seen as a gray area in terms of its legality, with some states deeming it illegal while others allowed it to operate. However, in recent years, a number of states have passed legislation explicitly legalizing and regulating DFS. This has helped to create a more stable and predictable regulatory environment for operators and players alike.

The Appeal of Skill-Based Gaming

Daily fantasy sports have also become popular because they are considered to be skill-based gaming. Unlike traditional sports betting, which is based largely on luck, DFS requires a significant amount of skill and strategy. Players must analyze player and team statistics, identify favorable matchups, and make strategic decisions based on their knowledge of the game. This appeal of skill-based gaming has attracted a large and growing number of players to the DFS industry.

High Prize Pools and Big Wins

Another key factor driving the growth of daily fantasy sports is the high prize pools and big wins that are available to players. DFS operators offer daily and weekly contests with prize pools ranging from a few thousand dollars to millions of dollars. This has created a sense of excitement and anticipation among players, who are drawn to the possibility of winning big and changing their lives.

The Rise of Fantasy Sports Culture

Finally, the growth of daily fantasy sports can be attributed in part to the rise of fantasy sports culture. Fantasy sports have become a cultural phenomenon, with millions of people around the world playing in seasonal leagues, participating in draft parties, and discussing player and team statistics on social media and online forums. The popularity of fantasy sports has helped to create a dedicated and passionate community of fans, many of whom have been drawn to daily fantasy sports as a way to further engage with the game.

In conclusion, the growth of daily fantasy sports can be attributed to a combination of technological advances, increased legalization and regulation, the appeal of skill-based gaming, high prize pools and big wins, and the rise of fantasy sports culture. As the industry continues to evolve and mature, it is likely that we will see even more innovation and growth in the years to come.

Women in Football

Football, also known as soccer, has historically been a male-dominated sport, with limited opportunities for women to participate and compete at the highest levels. However, in recent years, there has been a growing movement to promote and support women's football, both on and off the field. Below we will we will explore the history of women in football, the current state of the game, and the challenges and opportunities facing female players, coaches, and administrators.

A Brief History of Women in Football

Women have been playing football for over a century, with the first recorded women's football match taking place in 1895 in Edinburgh, Scotland. However, for many years, women's football was largely marginalized and ignored by the male-dominated sports establishment. In the early 20th century, several women's teams were formed in England and other countries, but they faced significant opposition and discrimination from the authorities and the media.

It was not until the 1960s and 1970s that women's football began to gain more recognition and support. The first Women's World Cup was held in 1970, but it was not officially recognized by FIFA until 1991. Since then, women's football has continued to grow and evolve, with the formation of professional leagues and the increased participation of women at all levels of the game.

The Current State of Women's Football

Today, women's football is more popular and visible than ever before, with millions of fans around the world watching and supporting their favorite teams and players. The Women's World Cup, held every four years, is now one of the biggest and most-watched sporting events in the world, with the 2019 tournament attracting a record-breaking audience of over 1 billion viewers.

In addition to the international tournaments, there are now professional women's leagues in many countries, including the United States, England, Germany, and France. These leagues offer female players the opportunity to compete at the highest levels of the game, earn a living wage, and build a career in football.

Challenges and Opportunities for Women in Football

Despite the progress that has been made in recent years, women in football still face a number of challenges and obstacles. One of the biggest challenges is the lack of investment and resources in women's football, both at the professional and grassroots levels. Many women's teams and leagues struggle to attract sponsors, fans, and media attention, which can limit their ability to grow and succeed.

Another challenge is the persistent gender bias and discrimination that female players and coaches face, both on and off the field. Women in football often have to work harder and prove themselves more than their male counterparts, and they may face obstacles in terms of access to coaching and leadership positions.

Despite these challenges, there are also many opportunities for women in football. As the game continues to grow and evolve, there are increasing opportunities for female players, coaches, and administrators to make their mark and help shape the future of the sport. Women's football is also becoming an important tool for promoting gender equality and empowerment, and for breaking down barriers and stereotypes.

In conclusion, women's football has come a long way since its humble beginnings in the late 19th century. Today, women's football is a global phenomenon, with millions of fans, players, and supporters around the world. While there are still challenges and obstacles to overcome, the future looks bright for women in football, as the game continues to evolve and grow, and more and more opportunities become available for female players, coaches, and administrators.

Female players and coaches

Women have made significant strides in the world of football in recent years, both as players and coaches. While there is still a long way to go in terms of achieving gender equality and representation, there are many talented and skilled female athletes and coaches who are making their mark on the sport. Below we will we will explore the history and current state of female players and coaches in football, the challenges they face, and the opportunities for growth and advancement in the sport.

History of Female Players in Football

Women have been playing football for over a century, but for much of that time, they faced significant discrimination and marginalization in the male-dominated sports establishment. It wasn't until the 1960s and 1970s that women's football began to gain more recognition and support, with the formation of international tournaments and leagues.

The Women's World Cup, first held in 1970, has played a key role in promoting and developing women's football around the world. The tournament has grown in popularity and importance over the years, with the 2019 event attracting a record-breaking audience of over 1 billion viewers.

Today, there are professional women's leagues in many countries, including the United States, England, Germany, and France. These leagues offer female players the opportunity to compete at the highest levels of the game, earn a living wage, and build a career in football.

Challenges and Opportunities for Female Players

Despite the progress that has been made in recent years, female players still face many challenges and obstacles in the world of football. One of the biggest challenges is the lack of investment and resources in women's football, which can limit the growth and development of the sport.

Female players may also face gender bias and discrimination in terms of pay, media coverage, and access to opportunities and resources. This can make it harder for female players to build successful careers in football, and can limit their ability to inspire and serve as role models for future generations of female players.

However, there are also many opportunities for female players in football. As the sport continues to grow and evolve, there are increasing opportunities for female players to make their mark and help shape the future of the game. Female players can serve as ambassadors for the sport, helping to inspire and empower other women to get involved and pursue their dreams.

History of Female Coaches in Football

Female coaches have also made significant contributions to the world of football, but they too have faced many challenges and obstacles along the way. Historically, women have been underrepresented in coaching and leadership positions in football, with most coaching roles being filled by men.

However, in recent years, there has been a growing movement to promote and support female coaches in football. This has led to the formation of initiatives and programs aimed at increasing the number of female coaches and providing them with the training and support they need to succeed.

Today, there are many talented and skilled female coaches working in football, both at the professional and grassroots levels. These coaches bring unique perspectives and experiences to the game, and they can serve as important role models and mentors for female players.

Challenges and Opportunities for Female Coaches

Female coaches still face many challenges and obstacles in the world of football. One of the biggest challenges is the persistent gender bias and discrimination that female coaches may face, both in terms of access to coaching opportunities and in terms of being taken seriously and respected as coaches.

Female coaches may also face challenges in terms of balancing their coaching careers with other responsibilities, such as family and personal commitments.

However, there are also many opportunities for female coaches in football. As the sport continues to evolve and grow, there is an increasing demand for skilled and knowledgeable coaches who can help guide and develop the next generation of football players.

Growth of women's leagues

The growth of women's leagues in football has been a relatively recent phenomenon. While women have been playing football since the early 20th century, it wasn't until the 1970s that organized women's football began to emerge. Since then, the sport has grown in popularity and has seen the creation of several professional and semi-professional leagues.

One of the earliest women's football leagues was the Women's Professional Football League (WPFL), which was founded in 1999. The league operated for several years before folding in 2008 due to financial difficulties. In 2009, the Women's Football Alliance (WFA) was founded, and it quickly became the largest women's football league in the United States. The league has over 60 teams and more than 2,000 players.

In addition to the WFA, there is also the Independent Women's Football League (IWFL), which was founded in 2000. The IWFL has teams throughout the United States, Canada, and Europe, and it has been instrumental in promoting women's football on an international level.

One of the challenges facing women's football is the lack of media coverage and support from major sponsors. This has led to a situation where many women's teams struggle to attract players and sponsors, which in turn makes it difficult for the leagues to grow and develop.

Despite these challenges, women's football has seen significant growth in recent years. The sport has been added to the Olympic program, and several countries have established national teams. The United States Women's National Football Team (USWNT) has been particularly successful, winning the World Cup on four occasions.

Women have also made inroads into coaching and officiating in football. In 2021, Jennifer King became the first full-time female assistant coach in NFL history, working with the Washington Football Team. Sarah Thomas became the first female official to work a Super Bowl in 2021 as well.

The growth of women's football is a positive development for the sport, and it is likely that we will see further growth and development in the coming years. With increased media coverage and support from sponsors, women's football has the potential to become a major force in the world of sports.

Pioneers and trailblazers

Throughout the history of football, there have been numerous pioneers and trailblazers who have made significant contributions to the sport. These individuals have helped to shape the game and have paved the way for future generations of players and coaches.

One of the earliest pioneers in football was Walter Camp. Considered by many to be the father of American football, Camp is credited with developing many of the basic rules and principles of the game. He was instrumental in establishing the first football programs at several universities, including Yale and Stanford, and he helped to standardize the size and shape of the football.

Another important figure in the early history of football was Amos Alonzo Stagg. Stagg was a player and coach at the University of Chicago and is widely regarded as one of the most innovative and influential coaches in the history of the sport. He introduced a number of new strategies and techniques, including the lateral pass and the T formation, and he was a vocal advocate for player safety.

In the early days of football, the sport was almost exclusively played by men. However, there were a few trailblazing women who helped to break down barriers and pave the way for future female players. One of the most notable of these women was Bertha Benz, who played football in Germany in the late 19th century. Another important figure was Rosalind Wiener Wyman, who helped to establish the first women's tackle football league in the United States in the 1970s.

As the sport of football continued to evolve, so too did the role of coaches. One of the most influential coaches of the modern era is Bill Walsh. Walsh was the head coach of the San Francisco 49ers during their dynasty in the 1980s, and he is credited with developing the West Coast offense, which revolutionized the way that the game is played.

Another important figure in the world of football coaching is Tony Dungy. Dungy was the first African-American head coach to win a Super Bowl, leading the Indianapolis Colts to victory in 2007. He is also known for his emphasis on character and integrity, and he has been a vocal advocate for diversity and inclusion in the coaching ranks.

In recent years, there has been a growing recognition of the role that women have played in football. In addition to the pioneers mentioned earlier, there have been several women who have made significant contributions to the sport in recent years. One of the most notable of these is Jen Welter, who became the first woman to coach in the NFL when she was hired as an assistant coach by the Arizona Cardinals in 2015.

Another important figure in the world of women's football is Sam Rapoport. Rapoport is the senior director of diversity and inclusion for the NFL, and she has been instrumental in promoting and advancing the cause of women in football. She has worked to establish programs and initiatives aimed at increasing the number of women coaches, scouts, and front office personnel in the league.

Finally, it is worth mentioning the many players who have broken down barriers and shattered records throughout the history of football. From Jim Thorpe, the first Native American to win an Olympic gold medal and a professional football championship, to Tom Brady, the winningest quarterback in NFL history, these players have helped to shape the sport and inspire future generations of players.

In conclusion, the history of football is rich with pioneers and trailblazers who have made significant contributions to the sport. From the early days of the game to the present day, these individuals have helped to shape the way that football is played and enjoyed. Their legacy serves as a reminder of the power of innovation, determination, and perseverance, and their impact will be felt for generations to come.

Future of Football

Football has been a staple of American sports culture for over a century. However, like any other sport, it has evolved over time to adapt to the changing times and demands of the modern world. As we look towards the future of football, there are a few key trends and developments that are likely to shape the game in the coming years.

One of the biggest trends in football right now is the growing concern around player safety. In recent years, there has been a lot of attention paid to the long-term effects of concussions and other head injuries that players sustain over the course of their careers. As a result, there has been a lot of research done to try and develop new technologies and techniques that can help reduce the risk of injury on the field.

One example of this is the increased use of helmet sensors, which can help track the number and severity of hits that players take during a game. This information can then be used to help coaches and medical staff better understand the risks that players are facing, and take steps to prevent injuries from occurring.

Another area where we are likely to see a lot of growth in the coming years is in the use of data and analytics. With so much data now available on every aspect of the game, from player performance to game strategy, there is a huge opportunity to use this information to gain a competitive advantage.

We are already starting to see this in the way that teams approach player evaluations and the draft. Rather than relying solely on traditional scouting methods, many teams are now using advanced data analytics to identify players who may have been overlooked by other teams, or who have hidden potential that has yet to be fully realized.

Similarly, we are likely to see a lot more innovation in terms of game strategy and play calling. With so much data now available on the strengths and weaknesses of different players and teams, coaches and offensive coordinators are increasingly using this information to develop more creative and effective plays that can exploit these weaknesses.

One area where we are already seeing a lot of experimentation is in the use of new formations and personnel groupings. For example, some teams are now using more spread formations to create mismatches with opposing defenses, while others are using more versatile players who can line up in a variety of different positions to keep defenses guessing.

Finally, there is the question of how football will adapt to the changing media landscape. With more and more people cutting the cord and ditching traditional cable TV, there is a growing need for sports leagues to find new ways to reach their audiences.

One area where we are likely to see a lot of growth in the coming years is in the use of streaming services and digital platforms. Already, many leagues are experimenting with new ways to deliver their content online, from live streaming games to creating more interactive and engaging fan experiences.

Overall, the future of football is likely to be shaped by a combination of technological innovation, data analytics, and changing media trends. While the core elements of the game may remain the same, we can expect to see a lot of exciting changes and developments in the coming years as the sport continues to evolve to meet the needs and expectations of modern fans.

Technological advancements

Technological advancements have played a significant role in shaping the game of football over the years. From instant replay to advanced analytics, technology has allowed players, coaches, and fans to experience the game in new and exciting ways.

One of the most significant technological advancements in football is the introduction of instant replay. Instant replay allows officials to review certain calls on the field, providing a second look at controversial plays. This technology has become an integral part of the game, helping to ensure that the correct calls are made on the field. In addition, instant replay has led to a greater level of transparency in the game, allowing fans to see the plays that officials are reviewing and to make their own judgments about the calls.

Another significant technological advancement in football is the use of advanced analytics. With the help of computer programs and algorithms, coaches and players can now analyze game data in new and innovative ways. This data can be used to help coaches develop game plans, evaluate player performance, and make strategic decisions during games. In addition, fans can also use this data to gain a deeper understanding of the game and to make more informed decisions when placing bets on games.

The use of technology has also led to significant improvements in player safety. In recent years, the NFL has implemented new rules and regulations designed to reduce the risk of concussions and other head injuries. Additionally, new equipment such as helmets and pads have been developed to better protect players on the field. These advancements have helped to reduce the number of serious injuries on the field and have made the game safer for players at all levels.

One area where technology is rapidly advancing is in the field of virtual reality. Virtual reality technology allows players to experience the game in new and exciting ways, providing a realistic and immersive experience that can help players improve their skills and gain a better understanding of the game. In addition, virtual reality technology can also be used to help fans experience the game in new ways, such as providing a 360-degree view of the action on the field.

As technology continues to advance, there is no doubt that it will play an even greater role in the game of football. From improvements in player safety to advancements in analytics and virtual reality, technology will continue to shape the way the game is played and experienced by players and fans alike.

Player safety and rule changes

Player safety has become a major focus in the world of football over the past few decades. With the increased awareness of the long-term effects of concussions and other head injuries, the NFL and other football organizations have taken significant steps to improve player safety on the field.

One of the most significant changes in recent years has been the implementation of new rules designed to reduce the risk of head injuries. For example, the NFL has instituted strict rules regarding helmet-to-helmet contact and other types of dangerous hits. These rules are designed to protect players from serious head injuries and to promote a safer style of play on the field.

Another area where significant progress has been made in improving player safety is in the development of new equipment. Over the past few decades, new helmets, pads, and other protective gear have been developed to better protect players on the field. For example, modern football helmets are designed to absorb the impact of hits and reduce the risk of head injuries. Similarly, new padding technology has been developed to reduce the risk of injuries to other parts of the body, such as the knees and shoulders.

In addition to these changes, many football organizations have also implemented new protocols for diagnosing and treating concussions. These protocols are designed to ensure that players receive prompt and appropriate medical attention in the event of a head injury. In some cases, players may be required to undergo a series of tests and evaluations before being allowed to return to the field.

While these changes have helped to make the game safer for players, there is still more work to be done. Some experts argue that the NFL and other organizations need to do more to protect players from the long-term effects of head injuries, such as chronic traumatic encephalopathy (CTE). Others argue that the rules changes and other safety measures have made the game less exciting for fans, and that a balance needs to be struck between player safety and the entertainment value of the game.

Despite these challenges, it is clear that player safety will continue to be a major focus in the world of football for years to come. As new technologies and strategies are developed, it is likely that even more effective safety measures will be implemented to protect players on the field. And as the game continues to evolve, it is important that players, coaches, and fans all work together to ensure that football remains a safe and exciting sport for generations to come.

Global expansion and international competitions

Football is a global sport, with millions of fans and players around the world. While the sport is most popular in North America and Europe, it is also gaining popularity in other parts of the world. Over the past few decades, the NFL and other football organizations have made significant efforts to expand the reach of the sport and to promote international competitions.

One of the most visible examples of this international expansion has been the growth of the NFL's annual international games. Starting in 2007, the NFL began playing regular season games outside of North America, with games being played in London, Mexico City, and other cities around the world. These games have been a major success, with millions of fans tuning in to watch the games and thousands of fans traveling from around the world to attend in person.

In addition to these regular season games, the NFL has also launched the NFL International Series, which is designed to promote the sport of football around the world. This series includes a range of events and programs, including youth football camps, coaching clinics, and player appearances. Through these programs, the NFL hopes to inspire the next generation of football players and fans around the world.

The NFL is not the only football organization that has been working to promote the sport globally. The International Federation of American Football (IFAF) is a non-profit organization that promotes the sport of football outside of North America. The IFAF has more than 100 member countries and works to develop the sport in regions around the world.

One of the key initiatives of the IFAF has been the development of international competitions, such as the World Championship of American Football. These competitions bring together teams from around the world to compete against each other and showcase the best of the sport on a global stage.

Other football organizations, such as the Canadian Football League (CFL) and the Arena Football League (AFL), have also been working to expand the reach of the sport outside of North America. The CFL has held games in the United States and has also explored the possibility of expanding into international markets, while the AFL has launched an international league to promote the sport in other parts of the world.

As football continues to grow in popularity around the world, there are many challenges that must be addressed. One of the biggest challenges is developing the infrastructure and resources needed to support the sport in other countries. This includes building new stadiums, developing training facilities, and attracting sponsors and media partners to support the sport.

Another challenge is adapting the sport to the unique cultural and social contexts of different regions around the world. For example, in some countries, the sport may need to be adapted to local rules and regulations, or may need to be promoted in different ways to appeal to local audiences.

Despite these challenges, the future of football looks bright. With millions of fans and players around the world, and with organizations like the NFL, IFAF, and others working to promote the sport globally, there is no doubt that football will continue to grow in popularity in the years to come. And as the sport continues to evolve and expand, it will continue to bring people together from all corners of the globe in the shared love of the game.

Flag Football and Alternative Formats

Flag football is a version of American football that is played without any physical contact between players. Instead of tackling, players must remove a flag from the ball carrier's waist to stop the play. Flag football is gaining in popularity around the world, with both casual and competitive leagues available for players of all ages and skill levels. In addition to flag football, there are several alternative formats of the game that are gaining popularity, such as touch football and ultimate football. Below we will we will explore the history and evolution of flag football and alternative formats, their rules and gameplay, and their increasing popularity among players and fans.

Flag football has been around since the early 1900s, and its popularity has increased in recent years, particularly as a safer alternative to tackle football. The game is typically played on a field that is smaller than a standard football field, with a team consisting of five to seven players on each side. The objective of the game is to score touchdowns by carrying the ball across the opponent's goal line. However, instead of tackling, players wear flags attached to their waistbands, and opponents must remove the flags to end the play.

The rules of flag football are similar to those of tackle football, with a few key differences. For example, instead of a kickoff, the game begins with a coin toss to determine which team will receive the ball first. The game is played in two 20-minute halves, with a running clock that stops only for injuries, timeouts, and incomplete passes in the final two minutes of each half.

Another key difference between flag and tackle football is the way in which scoring is calculated. In flag football, a touchdown is worth six points, and teams have the option to go for either one or two extra points after a touchdown. A one-point conversion is attempted from the five-yard line, while a two-point conversion is attempted from the 10-yard line. Additionally, field goals are worth three points, and a safety is worth two points.

Flag football is also played with a set of specific rules and guidelines that are designed to ensure player safety. For example, players are prohibited from blocking below the waist, and stiff-arming and tackling are not allowed. Additionally, players must wear mouthguards and are required to wear flags at all times during the game.

In addition to flag football, there are several alternative formats of the game that are gaining in popularity. One such format is touch football, which is similar to flag football but requires players to be touched by an opponent rather than having their flags removed. Another format is ultimate football, which is played with a flying disc rather than a football. The rules of ultimate football are similar to those of ultimate frisbee, with players attempting to score by catching the disc in an end zone.

One of the main benefits of flag football and other alternative formats is that they offer a safer alternative to tackle football, particularly for children and young adults. In recent years, there has been growing concern over the long-term health effects of concussions and other head injuries that are common in tackle football. By eliminating contact from the game, flag football and other alternative formats help to reduce the risk of serious injury while still providing players with the opportunity to participate in a fun and competitive sport.

Another benefit of flag football and other alternative formats is that they are more accessible to players of all ages and skill levels. Unlike tackle football, which requires a significant amount of strength, speed, and athleticism, flag football can be played by anyone, regardless of their physical abilities. This makes it a great option for players who are looking for a fun and low-impact way to stay active and stay involved in sports.

As a result of these benefits, flag football and other alternative formats are becoming increasingly popular around the world. There are now numerous flag football leagues and tournaments available.

Differences from traditional football

Flag football is a popular alternative format of football, especially for those who may not be interested in the physicality of traditional football or who are looking for a more accessible version of the game. Unlike traditional football, flag football is played with a flag belt worn around the waist of each player, and the objective is to remove the flag of the opposing player to stop the play.

One of the significant differences between flag football and traditional football is the contact allowed during the game. While traditional football involves physical contact, flag football emphasizes speed, agility, and precision. In flag football, players cannot make physical contact with one another, and instead, the game is played by grabbing the flag belt of the opposing player to stop the play.

Another significant difference between flag football and traditional football is the number of players on the field. Flag football is played with fewer players on the field, typically six or seven players per team, as opposed to the eleven players per team in traditional football. This smaller team size enables players to be more involved in the game, and there is less congestion on the field.

The field size in flag football is also smaller than traditional football. A standard flag football field measures 80 yards in length and 40 yards in width, while a standard traditional football field is 100 yards in length and 50 yards in width. This smaller field size also allows for a faster pace of play and quicker decision-making on the part of the players.

Flag football also has different rules regarding how a player can advance the ball. In traditional football, the ball can be advanced by either running or passing, while in flag football, only passing is allowed. Additionally, flag football games often have rules regarding the number of plays allowed per possession, the length of the game, and the use of timeouts.

One of the significant advantages of flag football is its accessibility. Since the game does not involve physical contact, it can be played by people of all ages and skill levels, making it an excellent alternative for those who may not be interested in the physicality of traditional football. Flag football can be played as a recreational sport or as a competitive sport in leagues and tournaments.

Flag football has gained popularity in recent years and is played worldwide, with national and international competitions held regularly. The International Flag Football Federation (IFFF) was established in 2002 and has over 40 member nations worldwide. The IFFF organizes international competitions, including the World Flag Football Championships, and has helped to promote the sport globally.

There are also other alternative formats of football, including touch football and indoor football, which are played with different rules and in different settings. Touch football is similar to flag football in that players cannot make physical contact, but instead of wearing flag belts, players must touch their opponents to stop the play. Indoor football is played on a smaller field, usually indoors, and emphasizes quickness, agility, and precise passing.

Strategies and gameplay

Flag football is a popular variation of traditional football that has grown in popularity in recent years. Unlike tackle football, where players are tackled to the ground, flag football involves removing a flag attached to the ball carrier's waist to signify a "tackle." This format is particularly appealing for those who want to play football without the physical contact and injuries that come with tackle football. Below we will we will explore the strategies and gameplay involved in flag football.

One of the main differences between flag football and traditional football is the number of players on the field. While traditional football is played with eleven players on each side, flag football is usually played with only five or six players on each team. The smaller field size and the reduced number of players create a faster-paced game with more opportunities for players to make big plays.

Another key difference in flag football is the way that players line up on the field. In traditional football, players are assigned specific positions and line up accordingly. In flag football, however, players can line up anywhere on the field as long as they are not in the neutral zone, which is usually one yard behind the line of scrimmage. This allows for more creative play calling and can catch opposing teams off guard.

The offensive strategy in flag football revolves around using the field's width to create mismatches and exploit gaps in the defense. This is achieved through a variety of passing plays, such as the quick pass, screen pass, and deep pass. The quarterback is the key player on the offensive side and is responsible for delivering accurate passes to the receivers. The receivers, meanwhile, need to run precise routes and use their speed and agility to create separation from the defenders.

To make it more difficult for the defense to anticipate the play, offenses often use motion before the snap. This involves a player moving before the ball is snapped, which can confuse the defense and create openings for the offense to exploit. Additionally, teams can use different formations, such as the trips formation or spread formation, to create unique matchups and exploit the defense's weaknesses.

On the defensive side, the key to success is to limit the offense's ability to create big plays. This is achieved through a variety of strategies, including man-to-man coverage, zone coverage, and blitzing. In man-to-man coverage, each defender is responsible for covering a specific offensive player. In zone coverage, each defender is responsible for covering a specific area of the field. Blitzing involves sending additional defenders to rush the quarterback, which can disrupt the offensive flow and create opportunities for turnovers.

One of the most important defensive strategies in flag football is "bump and run." This involves the defender making contact with the receiver at the line of scrimmage, which can disrupt their timing and create openings for the defense. Additionally, the defense can use stunts, where defenders swap positions before the snap, to confuse the offensive line and create openings for a sack or interception.

Another unique aspect of flag football is the use of the "double pass." This is where the quarterback throws the ball to a receiver, who then throws the ball to another receiver downfield. This play is particularly effective when the defense is expecting a standard passing play and can create big gains for the offense.

In terms of gameplay, flag football games usually consist of two halves, each lasting around 20-25 minutes. The clock stops on incomplete passes and when a player goes out of bounds, which means that the game can be extended if the offense can keep completing passes. Overtime periods are usually played in a "sudden death" format, where the first team to score wins the game.

Growing popularity

Flag football is a variation of American football that eliminates some of the physical contact and tackles involved in traditional football. It has gained immense popularity in recent years as an alternative to full-contact football, with many players opting for flag football as a safer and more accessible option. Below we will explore the growing popularity of flag football and why it has become an attractive alternative to traditional football.

One of the main reasons for the growing popularity of flag football is safety concerns. Football has been known for its violent collisions and head injuries, which can cause severe long-term damage to players. Flag football provides a less physical and safer environment for players who may not want to risk getting hurt in full-contact football. This is especially important for youth players who may not have developed the physical strength and endurance necessary for contact football. Flag football also allows players who have experienced injuries to continue playing the sport they love without risking further injury.

Another reason for the popularity of flag football is its accessibility. Traditional football requires a large field and expensive equipment, making it difficult for many people to play. On the other hand, flag football can be played in a smaller field with minimal equipment requirements, making it easier for people of all ages and skill levels to participate. This has led to an increase in the number of recreational leagues, tournaments, and pickup games, making it a popular choice for those looking for a fun and social way to stay active.

Flag football has also gained popularity due to the rise of women's sports. Many women who want to play football are often discouraged by the physical demands of the sport, leading them to seek out alternatives like flag football. With women's leagues and tournaments popping up all over the country, flag football has become a viable option for women who want to compete and stay active.

The growing popularity of flag football has also led to its inclusion in high schools and colleges across the country. Many schools have adopted flag football as an alternative to tackle football, allowing more students to participate in the sport while reducing the risk of injuries. This has led to an increase in the number of scholarships and opportunities for students who want to continue playing football at the collegiate level.

In addition, the popularity of flag football has given rise to new formats and variations of the game. One popular format is 7-on-7 flag football, which is played with seven players on each team instead of the traditional 11. This allows for a faster and more dynamic game, with more opportunities for passing and scoring. Another variation is coed flag football, which allows men and women to play on the same team, promoting gender equality and inclusivity.

Overall, the popularity of flag football is driven by its safety, accessibility, and versatility. It provides a fun and social way to stay active while still playing the sport of football. With the growth of recreational leagues, high school and college programs, and new variations of the game, it is clear that flag football is here to stay.

Youth Football and Player Development

Youth football is an essential component of player development in American football. The sport provides an opportunity for young athletes to develop their physical abilities, learn the fundamentals of the game, and build important life skills such as teamwork, discipline, and perseverance. Below we will explore the importance of youth football in player development, the challenges that the sport faces, and the ways that youth football can continue to grow and thrive.

The Benefits of Youth Football

Youth football provides numerous benefits to young athletes. For one, it teaches important physical skills such as running, jumping, and throwing, all of which are essential components of football. Furthermore, the sport encourages healthy habits such as exercise, healthy eating, and hydration. Youth football also provides a valuable opportunity for young athletes to develop important social skills such as communication, teamwork, and leadership. These skills are critical not just in football, but in life in general.

Youth football can also serve as a stepping stone to higher levels of play. Many successful NFL players got their start in youth football, and the skills and experience that they gained at the youth level helped prepare them for success later in their careers.

Challenges Facing Youth Football

Despite the benefits of youth football, the sport faces several challenges. One of the primary concerns is player safety. There is growing concern about the long-term effects of head injuries and concussions in football, and many parents are hesitant to allow their children to participate in the sport. Additionally, the cost of playing football can be prohibitive for some families, especially in low-income areas where access to resources is limited.

Another challenge facing youth football is the lack of diversity. The sport has traditionally been dominated by white athletes, and there are relatively few opportunities for players from underrepresented groups to participate. This lack of diversity not only deprives the sport of valuable talent but also reinforces harmful stereotypes and biases.

Ways to Improve Youth Football

To address the challenges facing youth football, several strategies can be implemented. First, the sport needs to take player safety seriously. This means implementing strict safety protocols, providing appropriate training and equipment, and ensuring that coaches are trained to recognize and respond to potential injuries.

Second, youth football needs to become more accessible to underrepresented groups. This means providing resources and support to low-income families and creating programs specifically targeted at recruiting and developing players from diverse backgrounds.

Third, youth football needs to adapt to changes in the sport. As technology advances and the game evolves, youth football needs to adapt its strategies and training programs accordingly. This may mean implementing new training techniques, introducing new equipment, and rethinking the structure of the game itself.

Youth football is a critical component of player development in American football. The sport provides an opportunity for young athletes to develop important physical and social skills, and it can serve as a stepping stone to higher levels of play. However, the sport faces several challenges, including concerns about player safety and lack of diversity. To address these challenges, youth football needs to take player safety seriously, become more accessible to underrepresented groups, and adapt to changes in the sport. By doing so, youth football can continue to thrive and provide valuable opportunities for young athletes for generations to come.

Importance of fundamentals

Football is a physically demanding sport that requires skill, coordination, and teamwork to be successful. As with any sport, the foundation for success begins with mastering the fundamentals, particularly for young players. Youth football provides a unique opportunity for children to develop their skills and gain confidence, both on and off the field. Below we will we will discuss the importance of fundamentals in youth football and how they contribute to player development.

Fundamentals refer to the basic skills and techniques required to play football, including throwing, catching, blocking, tackling, and running. These skills are essential for all players, regardless of their position on the field, and they form the foundation for more advanced techniques and strategies. The development of these skills is critical for the success of the individual player, as well as the team as a whole.

One of the most significant benefits of youth football is that it provides young athletes with the opportunity to learn and practice these fundamentals in a controlled and safe environment. Coaches and trainers can work with players to develop their skills and technique through a variety of drills and exercises. They can also teach players proper form and technique for each skill, which is crucial for avoiding injuries and developing good habits that will carry over into the game.

In addition to the physical benefits of developing fundamental skills, youth football also provides young athletes with valuable life lessons. The discipline, hard work, and teamwork required to succeed in football can translate to success in other areas of life, such as academics and careers. Players also learn the importance of sportsmanship and fair play, as well as how to handle both success and failure with grace and humility.

Another benefit of youth football is that it provides young athletes with the opportunity to develop a love and passion for the sport. Football can be an intimidating and challenging sport, but with the right guidance and support, players can develop the skills and confidence necessary to enjoy the game. Many players find that the discipline and focus required to succeed in football carry over into other areas of their lives, leading to increased self-esteem and a sense of purpose.

It is important to note that youth football is not without its risks. As with any contact sport, there is always a risk of injury, particularly when players are not properly trained or equipped. However, by focusing on the fundamentals and emphasizing safe and responsible play, coaches and trainers can minimize these risks and ensure that young athletes have a positive and rewarding experience.

In recent years, there has been growing concern about the long-term effects of football-related injuries, particularly concussions. While the risk of concussion is present in all levels of football, it is particularly concerning for young athletes whose brains are still developing. To address this issue, many youth football organizations have implemented new rules and guidelines to promote safer play, such as limiting contact during practices and games and requiring the use of protective equipment.

Overall, youth football provides young athletes with a unique opportunity to develop their skills, build confidence, and learn valuable life lessons. By emphasizing the fundamentals and promoting safe and responsible play, coaches and trainers can help players not only succeed on the field but also in all areas of their lives. As the sport continues to evolve, it is important that we remain vigilant in our efforts to promote the health and well-being of our young athletes, while also fostering a love and passion for the game of football.

Safety concerns and rule adjustments

Football is a contact sport that involves physical exertion, and injuries are an inevitable part of the game. Safety is a primary concern in football, and coaches, players, and parents must take precautions to minimize the risk of injuries. Youth football is a popular activity, and many children participate in the sport. Therefore, safety measures are critical in promoting the development of young players and ensuring their safety.

There have been significant safety concerns related to football in recent years. A study published in the Journal of the American Medical Association found that professional football players were more likely to develop chronic traumatic encephalopathy (CTE), a neurodegenerative disease that can lead to cognitive and behavioral problems. CTE is thought to be caused by repeated blows to the head, which can occur during practices and games. This has led to an increased focus on safety measures in football, particularly at the youth level.

One significant step towards ensuring the safety of young football players has been the introduction of new rules and regulations. In recent years, the sport's governing bodies have made significant changes to the rules to minimize the risk of injuries. For example, the NFL has made significant changes to the rules regarding tackling, particularly targeting the head and neck. These changes aim to reduce the risk of concussions and other head injuries.

Additionally, football coaches have been encouraged to modify their practice routines to minimize the risk of injuries. For example, coaches have been encouraged to limit full-contact practices and to focus more on drills and other non-contact activities. This approach can help reduce the risk of injuries during practice, ensuring that young players remain healthy and can continue to develop their skills.

Another significant development in youth football has been the increased focus on player safety equipment. Helmets, pads, and other safety equipment have been designed and improved to provide better protection for young players. For example, helmets have been designed with better padding and a more secure fit to reduce the risk of head injuries. Similarly, pads have been developed with improved shock absorption properties, which can help reduce the risk of injuries to the torso and legs.

In addition to safety equipment, there has been a growing emphasis on player safety education. Coaches, parents, and players themselves have been encouraged to learn more about safety measures and best practices to minimize the risk of injuries. This education can help young players better understand the importance of safety and how to avoid common injuries.

Finally, youth football leagues have begun to focus on player development rather than just winning. This shift in focus has led to a more holistic approach to youth football, which emphasizes the importance of developing young players' skills and ensuring that they are healthy and safe. This approach has helped promote the long-term development of young players and has helped create a safer and more enjoyable environment for all involved.

Building a foundation for success

Building a foundation for success is essential in all aspects of life, and football is no exception. As one of the most physically demanding and mentally challenging sports, football requires players to have a strong foundation of fundamental skills, discipline, and dedication. Below we will we will explore the key elements that contribute to building a strong foundation for success in football.

One of the most important aspects of building a foundation for success in football is mastering the fundamental skills of the game. This includes proper technique for blocking, tackling, throwing, catching, and running. Coaches at all levels of the sport emphasize the importance of mastering these skills, as they form the basis for success on the field.

In addition to mastering the fundamentals, football players must also have discipline and dedication. This means adhering to a strict training regimen, maintaining a healthy diet, and staying focused on the team's goals. Players who lack discipline and dedication are unlikely to succeed at the highest levels of the sport, as the demands of football require a significant amount of mental and physical toughness.

Another important element of building a strong foundation for success in football is teamwork. Football is a team sport, and players must be able to work together effectively in order to achieve their goals. This means practicing together regularly, communicating effectively on the field, and supporting each other through the ups and downs of the season. Teams that lack a strong sense of unity and teamwork are unlikely to achieve success on the field.

In addition to mastering the fundamentals, discipline and dedication, and teamwork, football players must also have a strong work ethic. This means putting in the time and effort required to improve their skills, both on and off the field. Football players must be willing to sacrifice their time and energy in order to achieve their goals, and they must be willing to push themselves to the limits of their abilities in order to reach their full potential.

Another key element of building a strong foundation for success in football is mental toughness. Football is a physically demanding sport, but it is also mentally challenging. Players must be able to stay focused and maintain a positive attitude, even in the face of adversity. They must be able to stay calm under pressure, and they must be able to overcome setbacks and challenges in order to achieve their goals.

Finally, building a foundation for success in football requires a strong support system. This includes coaches, family, friends, and teammates who are all invested in the player's success. A strong support system can provide the encouragement and motivation that players need to overcome obstacles and stay focused on their goals.

Officiating and Rules

Officiating and rules are crucial components of football as they ensure fairness, safety, and consistency in the game. Football rules have evolved over the years and continue to be refined to accommodate new strategies, techniques, and technologies. Below we will we will explore the role of officiating and rules in football, how they are developed and implemented, and the controversies that have arisen in recent times.

Officiating refers to the individuals who enforce the rules of the game and make sure that players abide by them. These officials include referees, umpires, and linesmen, who work together to ensure that the game is played fairly and within the rules. The officials have a challenging task, as they have to make split-second decisions in a fast-paced and physically demanding environment.

The rules of football are developed by various organizations, including the National Football League (NFL), the National Collegiate Athletic Association (NCAA), and the International Football Association Board (IFAB). These organizations have committees that are responsible for reviewing and updating the rules to address emerging issues in the game.

The rules cover various aspects of the game, including field dimensions, equipment, player conduct, and scoring. For example, the dimensions of the field and the markings are strictly regulated to ensure consistency across different venues. The equipment rules stipulate the types of helmets, pads, and cleats that players can wear to protect themselves and their opponents. The rules governing player conduct cover issues such as taunting, unsportsmanlike behavior, and penalties for dangerous plays.

One of the most significant changes in recent times has been the focus on player safety. The NFL, in particular, has come under intense scrutiny over the years for its handling of concussions and other injuries. The league has introduced new rules to reduce the risk of head injuries, such as prohibiting helmet-to-helmet hits and targeting the head or neck area. The NFL has also implemented a concussion protocol that requires players to be evaluated by medical personnel if they exhibit symptoms of a concussion.

However, these rule changes have not been without controversy. Some players and coaches have criticized the new rules, arguing that they have made the game less physical and exciting. Others have raised concerns that the rules are not being consistently enforced, leading to confusion and frustration among players and fans alike.

Another area of contention is the use of technology in officiating. In recent years, leagues have begun using instant replay and other technologies to review questionable calls and ensure that the right decisions are made. While technology has helped to reduce errors and improve the accuracy of officiating, some have argued that it has also slowed down the game and removed some of the human element.

The role of referees and officials

In American football, the role of referees and officials is vital to ensure the fairness and safety of the game. They are responsible for enforcing the rules and regulations of the game, making sure that the players play within the boundaries of the field and maintain good sportsmanship throughout the game. Below we will we will discuss the role of referees and officials in American football.

Firstly, referees and officials are responsible for ensuring that the game is played within the rules and regulations of the league. This means that they must have a deep understanding of the rules and be able to apply them consistently and fairly throughout the game. The referees and officials are also responsible for ensuring that all equipment used during the game meets the standards set by the league. This includes helmets, pads, and other protective gear used by the players.

Secondly, referees and officials play a crucial role in maintaining the safety of the players. They monitor the field of play and make sure that the players are not engaging in dangerous or illegal activities that could cause injury. This includes monitoring the players' equipment and making sure that it is properly fastened and not causing any danger to the player wearing it. Referees and officials are also responsible for ensuring that players do not engage in rough play or unsportsmanlike conduct, which could result in injury to other players.

Thirdly, referees and officials are responsible for making calls during the game. This includes determining when a player is out of bounds, when a pass is incomplete, and when a player has committed a penalty. The referees and officials are also responsible for determining the outcome of close plays, such as whether a touchdown was scored or if a player's knee was down before he crossed the goal line.

Finally, referees and officials play a critical role in maintaining the integrity of the game. They ensure that the game is played fairly and that no team has an unfair advantage. This includes monitoring the behavior of coaches and players, ensuring that they do not engage in cheating or other unethical behavior. Referees and officials also have the authority to eject players or coaches from the game if they engage in serious misconduct.

In conclusion, referees and officials play an essential role in American football. They are responsible for ensuring that the game is played within the rules and regulations of the league, maintaining the safety of the players, making calls during the game, and maintaining the integrity of the game. Without referees and officials, the game of football would be chaotic and unsafe. It is important for players, coaches, and fans to respect the role of referees and officials and to work together to ensure that the game is played fairly and safely.

Common penalties and their consequences

Penalties are an integral part of football, serving as a means to enforce fair play and maintain the integrity of the game. In the NFL, there are over 20 different penalties that officials can call during a game, each with its own set of consequences. Below we will we will discuss some of the most common penalties in football and their impact on the game.

One of the most common penalties in football is holding. Holding occurs when an offensive player impedes the progress of a defender by grabbing onto them or using their body to block their path. Holding is a 10-yard penalty, meaning the offense will lose 10 yards from the spot of the foul. Holding can be a costly penalty, as it can negate big plays and put the offense in a difficult position to convert on third down.

Another common penalty in football is pass interference. Pass interference occurs when a defensive player interferes with the ability of an offensive player to catch a pass. This can happen through physical contact, such as pushing or grabbing, or through blocking the receiver's path to the ball. Pass interference is a spot foul, meaning the penalty is assessed at the point of the foul. If the foul occurs in the end zone, the ball is placed at the one-yard line. Pass interference can have a significant impact on the game, as it can result in a large gain or even a touchdown for the offense.

False start is another penalty that occurs frequently in football. False start occurs when an offensive player moves before the ball is snapped. False start is a 5-yard penalty, meaning the offense will lose 5 yards from the line of scrimmage. False start can be costly for the offense, as it puts them in a difficult position to convert on third down and can result in a loss of momentum.

In addition to the penalties discussed above, there are many other penalties that can be called in football, including roughing the passer, roughing the kicker, unsportsmanlike conduct, and delay of game. Each penalty has its own set of consequences, and it is up to the officials to determine if a penalty has occurred and what the appropriate penalty should be.

Penalties are an important aspect of football, as they serve to maintain the integrity of the game and ensure fair play. While penalties can be frustrating for players and fans alike, they are necessary to ensure that the game is played in a safe and fair manner. By understanding the most common penalties in football and their impact on the game, fans can gain a better appreciation for the sport and the role that penalties play in maintaining the integrity of the game.

Controversial calls and rules changes

Controversial calls and rules changes are an inevitable part of the game of football. Referees and officials make judgments based on their interpretation of the rules, which can often lead to disagreements between fans, players, and coaches. Over time, these controversies have led to rule changes aimed at improving player safety, reducing the number of penalties, and increasing the overall fairness of the game.

One of the most famous controversial calls in football history occurred during the 1972 AFC Divisional Playoff game between the Pittsburgh Steelers and the Oakland Raiders. With the Raiders leading by a score of 7-6, the Steelers attempted a last-minute drive to win the game. On fourth down, quarterback Terry Bradshaw threw a pass that was deflected by Raiders safety Jack Tatum and caught by Steelers running back Franco Harris, who ran for a touchdown. The play was controversial because it appeared that the ball had touched the ground before Harris caught it. However, the officials ruled that the catch was legal, and the play became known as the "Immaculate Reception."

In response to controversies like this, the NFL has made a number of rule changes over the years. One of the most significant was the introduction of instant replay in 1986. This allowed coaches to challenge certain calls on the field, and referees could review the play on a video monitor to determine if the call was correct. Instant replay has since been expanded to include more types of calls and has become an important tool for officials to ensure that the game is played fairly.

Another important rule change aimed at improving player safety was the introduction of the helmet-to-helmet contact penalty in 2010. This penalty is assessed when a player intentionally uses his helmet to make contact with another player's helmet, neck, or face. The penalty is meant to reduce the risk of head injuries, which have become a major concern in football in recent years.

In addition to rule changes, the NFL has also implemented new equipment and technology aimed at improving player safety. For example, players now wear helmets with better padding and shock-absorbing materials, and some players have started using mouthguards that are designed to reduce the risk of concussions. In addition, the NFL has invested in new technologies like virtual reality training systems and impact sensors that can track the force of hits on players.

Controversial calls and rules changes are not unique to the NFL. In college football, there have been many controversial calls over the years, including the "fifth down" game between Colorado and Missouri in 1990, when the referees mistakenly allowed Colorado an extra down, which they used to score the game-winning touchdown. In response to controversies like this, college football has also implemented changes to the rules and officiating.

One of the most significant changes in college football in recent years has been the introduction of targeting penalties. This penalty is assessed when a player makes contact with an opponent's head or neck area with his helmet, shoulder, or forearm. Players who receive a targeting penalty are ejected from the game and may also face additional sanctions. The targeting penalty is meant to reduce the risk of head injuries and has been credited with reducing the number of serious injuries in college football.

In addition to rule changes and equipment improvements, there has also been a growing emphasis on player safety and concussion awareness in football. In recent years, there has been increasing concern about the long-term effects of repeated head trauma, and many players have become advocates for better safety measures and more research into the effects of head injuries.

The Art of Playcalling

In football, playcalling refers to the strategy and tactics a coach uses to determine which plays the offense should run in a given situation. The art of playcalling is one of the most important aspects of football coaching, as it can often be the difference between success and failure on the field. A good playcaller must be able to read the game situation, anticipate what the defense is going to do, and then call a play that gives the offense the best chance to succeed.

There are many different factors that can influence a coach's playcalling decisions. These can include the score of the game, the time remaining on the clock, the field position of the ball, the down and distance, the weather conditions, and the strengths and weaknesses of both the offense and defense. A good playcaller must be able to take all of these factors into account and make the best decision based on the information available.

One of the most important skills for a playcaller is the ability to read the defense. This involves studying film of the opposing team and understanding their defensive tendencies, such as which formations and blitz packages they like to use in different situations. The playcaller must then use this information to predict how the defense will react to different offensive formations and plays, and call plays that exploit the defense's weaknesses.

Another key aspect of playcalling is game management. This involves making decisions about when to use timeouts, when to go for it on fourth down, and when to kick a field goal or go for a two-point conversion. These decisions can be influenced by a variety of factors, including the score of the game, the time remaining on the clock, and the field position of the ball.

There are many different types of offensive plays that a playcaller can choose from. Some of the most common types of plays include runs, passes, and play-action passes. Runs are designed to gain yards on the ground, while passes are designed to gain yards through the air. Play-action passes are a type of pass play that is designed to look like a run play, with the goal of fooling the defense and creating a big play downfield.

In addition to these basic types of plays, there are also many different variations and wrinkles that a playcaller can use to keep the defense off balance. These can include trick plays, such as reverses and flea flickers, as well as different formations and personnel groupings. The key to successful playcalling is to keep the defense guessing and to always have a counter move ready in case the defense makes an adjustment.

Of course, even the best playcalling can be undone by mistakes on the field. Turnovers, penalties, and missed assignments can all derail a drive and prevent the offense from scoring points. As such, a good playcaller must also be able to motivate and inspire their players, to keep them focused and disciplined even in the face of adversity.

In recent years, advances in technology have changed the way that playcalling is done in football. Many teams now use tablets or other electronic devices on the sideline to review game film and make adjustments in real time. This has allowed coaches to be more nimble in their playcalling and has helped to level the playing field between teams with more or less talented personnel.

Overall, the art of playcalling is one of the most important aspects of football coaching. A good playcaller must be able to read the game situation, anticipate the defense, and make the best decision based on the information available. By using a combination of film study, game management, and creativity, a great playcaller can elevate their team to new heights of success.

Balancing offensive and defensive strategies

In football, playcalling is an art that requires a deep understanding of both offensive and defensive strategies. The goal of playcalling is to create a cohesive game plan that can be executed on the field to gain an advantage over the opponent. This involves a careful balance of offensive and defensive strategies, as well as the ability to adjust the game plan based on the flow of the game.

Offensive Playcalling

Offensive playcalling is centered on scoring points and moving the ball down the field. The offense is led by the quarterback, who has the primary responsibility of directing the offensive strategy. The playcaller, typically the head coach or offensive coordinator, works with the quarterback to devise a game plan that utilizes the strengths of the team's offensive players while exploiting the weaknesses of the opposing defense.

The key to successful offensive playcalling is a combination of creativity and execution. The playcaller must be able to come up with innovative plays that catch the defense off-guard while ensuring that the players can execute them effectively. This requires an intimate understanding of the team's offensive personnel, including their strengths, weaknesses, and tendencies.

One of the most important aspects of offensive playcalling is the ability to balance the running and passing game. The running game is typically used to control the clock and wear down the defense, while the passing game is used to gain chunks of yardage and score quick touchdowns. The playcaller must find a balance between the two to keep the defense off-balance and prevent them from keying in on one aspect of the offense.

Defensive Playcalling

Defensive playcalling is focused on stopping the opposing team's offense and preventing them from scoring points. The defensive coordinator is responsible for devising a game plan that utilizes the strengths of the team's defensive players while exploiting the weaknesses of the opposing offense.

The key to successful defensive playcalling is adaptability. The defensive coordinator must be able to adjust the game plan based on the opposing team's offensive strategy and the flow of the game. This requires a deep understanding of the opposing offense, including their tendencies, strengths, and weaknesses.

One of the most important aspects of defensive playcalling is the ability to disguise coverages and blitz packages. By showing different looks pre-snap, the defense can confuse the opposing quarterback and prevent him from making accurate throws. The defensive coordinator must be able to anticipate the opposing offense's tendencies and adjust the coverage and blitz packages accordingly.

Balancing Offense and Defense

The most successful teams are able to balance their offensive and defensive strategies to create a cohesive game plan that can be executed on the field. This requires a deep understanding of both offensive and defensive playcalling, as well as the ability to adjust the game plan based on the flow of the game.

One of the keys to balancing offense and defense is to play to the strengths of the team's personnel. If the team has a dominant running back, for example, the playcaller may rely more heavily on the running game. If the team has a strong pass rush, the defensive coordinator may call more blitz packages.

Another key to balancing offense and defense is to be aggressive when the situation calls for it. This means taking calculated risks and being willing to adjust the game plan based on the score and time remaining in the game. For example, if the team is down by a touchdown in the fourth quarter, the playcaller may call for more aggressive plays to try and score quickly and tie the game.

Reading defenses and making adjustments

In football, the quarterback is the key player on the offensive side of the ball. One of the quarterback's essential tasks is to read the defense and make adjustments accordingly. This requires a deep understanding of the various defensive schemes that the opposing team might deploy.

The quarterback's ability to read defenses and make adjustments can significantly impact the game's outcome. If a quarterback can read the defense and adjust the offensive strategy accordingly, it can lead to a successful play and potentially a score. Conversely, if the quarterback fails to recognize the defense and make the necessary adjustments, it could lead to a failed play or even a turnover.

There are many different defensive schemes that teams can employ, but the most common ones include man-to-man coverage, zone coverage, and blitzing.

Man-to-Man Coverage

Man-to-man coverage is a defensive scheme in which each defensive player is responsible for covering a specific offensive player. This strategy is often used in passing situations and is designed to prevent the offense from completing a pass.

To combat man-to-man coverage, the quarterback must recognize which defensive player is covering each offensive player. This requires a thorough understanding of the opposing team's defensive personnel and their tendencies.

One way to attack man-to-man coverage is by using crossing routes. This involves two or more receivers crossing paths, which can create confusion for the defenders and create space for a receiver to get open.

Zone Coverage

Zone coverage is a defensive scheme in which each defender is responsible for covering a specific area of the field. This scheme is designed to prevent the offense from completing a pass by creating traffic in the passing lanes.

To beat zone coverage, the quarterback must recognize the areas of the field that the defenders are responsible for covering. This requires an understanding of the defensive scheme and the patterns of movement that defenders tend to make.

One way to attack zone coverage is by using route combinations that create holes in the coverage. For example, running a receiver through the middle of the field while another receiver runs a route underneath can create confusion for the defenders and open up space for a receiver to get open.

Blitzing

Blitzing is a defensive scheme in which extra defenders rush the quarterback to put pressure on him and prevent him from making a successful pass. This strategy is often used in passing situations and is designed to disrupt the offensive rhythm.

To combat a blitz, the quarterback must recognize which defenders are rushing and where the pressure is coming from. This requires quick decision-making and a willingness to throw the ball away if necessary.

One way to beat a blitz is by using quick passes and screens. This involves getting the ball out of the quarterback's hands quickly and into the hands of a receiver who can gain yards after the catch.

Making Adjustments

In addition to recognizing the defensive scheme, the quarterback must also be able to make adjustments on the fly. This requires the ability to read the defense quickly and make decisions about where to throw the ball or where to run.

One way to make adjustments is by using audibles. Audibles are changes to the offensive play call that are made at the line of scrimmage based on the defensive look. This can involve changing the play entirely or changing the route for a specific receiver.

Another way to make adjustments is by using hot reads. Hot reads are quick throws to a specific receiver who is designed to be the first read in a passing play. This is typically used to beat blitzes, as the hot read can quickly get the ball out of the quarterback's hands and into the hands of a receiver who is open.

The role of analytics

The use of analytics has become increasingly important in football over the years. It involves the collection and analysis of data to help teams make strategic decisions about everything from game planning to player evaluation. Analytics has revolutionized the way football is played, and teams are now leveraging data-driven insights to gain a competitive advantage.

The use of analytics in football began to gain traction in the early 2000s when teams started using data to evaluate player performance. The NFL introduced a program called "NFL Game Statistics and Information System," which provided teams with access to data that could be used to evaluate players and game strategy. The program was a big hit, and teams began to invest more resources into data analysis.

Today, analytics is used in almost every aspect of football, from player scouting to in-game strategy. One area where analytics has had a significant impact is in playcalling. Coaches and offensive coordinators now use data to help them make informed decisions about which plays to call based on the situation.

For example, a coach may use analytics to determine which plays are most effective in third-down situations. They may analyze data from previous games to see which plays had the highest success rates on third down. Armed with this information, the coach can create a game plan that includes a higher percentage of plays that have been successful in third-down situations.

Analytics is also used to evaluate player performance. Teams use data to measure a player's success rate in different situations, such as how often a wide receiver catches the ball when targeted or how effective a running back is at gaining yards after contact. This information can be used to help coaches make informed decisions about which players to play in certain situations.

One of the most significant ways analytics has impacted football is in the area of game preparation. Teams now have access to vast amounts of data about their opponents, including their offensive and defensive tendencies, player strengths and weaknesses, and even tendencies in certain situations, such as how often a team runs on third down.

This information is used to create game plans that exploit the weaknesses of the opposing team while taking advantage of their strengths. For example, a team may decide to focus on the run game if they know that their opponent has a weak run defense. They may also decide to target a specific defensive back if they know that they struggle in coverage.

Analytics is also used to help teams evaluate the risk-reward of different in-game decisions. For example, coaches may use data to determine when to go for it on fourth down or when to attempt a two-point conversion instead of kicking an extra point. By evaluating the probability of success versus the potential reward, coaches can make informed decisions that can have a significant impact on the outcome of the game.

Finally, analytics is used to evaluate team performance over the course of the season. Teams can use data to track their success rate in different situations, such as third down or red-zone opportunities. They can also evaluate their success rate against different types of defenses or offensive formations.

This information can be used to help coaches adjust their game plans and make strategic decisions that can improve team performance over the course of the season.

Iconic Stadiums and Venues

Football stadiums and venues have played a significant role in the history and culture of the sport. From historic fields to modern state-of-the-art arenas, they have become an integral part of the game's tradition and identity. These iconic stadiums and venues have hosted some of the most memorable games, moments, and events in football history. Below we will we will explore some of the most famous and iconic football stadiums and venues.

Lambeau Field

Lambeau Field, located in Green Bay, Wisconsin, is the home of the Green Bay Packers, one of the oldest and most successful franchises in NFL history. The stadium was opened in 1957 and has undergone several renovations over the years. It is known for its distinctive design, including its iconic "Lambeau Leap" tradition, in which Packers players jump into the stands to celebrate touchdowns with fans.

Rose Bowl

The Rose Bowl, located in Pasadena, California, is one of the oldest and most famous stadiums in college football. It is home to the annual Rose Bowl game, which has been played since 1902 and is one of the most prestigious and popular bowl games in the country. The stadium has also hosted several Super Bowls and World Cup matches and has a capacity of over 90,000.

Notre Dame Stadium

Notre Dame Stadium, located in South Bend, Indiana, is the home of the Notre Dame Fighting Irish football team. It is one of the most historic and iconic college football stadiums, known for its traditional design and atmosphere. The stadium has a capacity of over 80,000 and has hosted many memorable games and events, including the famous "Game of the Century" between Notre Dame and Michigan State in 1966.

AT&T Stadium

AT&T Stadium, located in Arlington, Texas, is one of the most modern and technologically advanced stadiums in the world. It is the home of the Dallas Cowboys and has a capacity of over 100,000. The stadium is known for its massive high-definition video screen, which stretches from one 20-yard line to the other, and its retractable roof.

Wembley Stadium

Wembley Stadium, located in London, England, is one of the most iconic and historic stadiums in the world. It has been the site of many famous events, including the 1966 World Cup final and the Olympic Games. The stadium has undergone several renovations over the years and has a capacity of over 90,000.

Michigan Stadium

Michigan Stadium, located in Ann Arbor, Michigan, is the home of the Michigan Wolverines football team. It is one of the largest stadiums in the world, with a capacity of over 107,000. The stadium is known for its unique design, including its bowl shape and the iconic Michigan "M" that is painted on the field.

Soldier Field

Soldier Field, located in Chicago, Illinois, is the home of the Chicago Bears football team. It has a rich history, dating back to the 1920s, and has undergone several renovations over the years. The stadium is known for its distinctive design, including its colonnades and the iconic "Soldier Statue" that stands outside the main entrance.

Los Angeles Memorial Coliseum

The Los Angeles Memorial Coliseum, located in Los Angeles, California, is one of the most historic and iconic stadiums in the country. It has been the site of many famous events, including two Olympic Games and several Super Bowls. The stadium is currently home to the USC Trojans football team and has a capacity of over 77,000.

Ohio Stadium

Ohio Stadium, located in Columbus, Ohio, is the home of the Ohio State Buckeyes football team.

Historic football stadiums

Football is one of the most popular sports in the world, and it has been played in many iconic and historic stadiums throughout its history. These stadiums have become symbols of the sport, and they have played a significant role in shaping the culture of football.

One of the most iconic football stadiums in the world is Wembley Stadium in London, England. Wembley was originally built in 1923, and it has undergone several renovations since then. The stadium has hosted some of the most important football matches in history, including the 1966 FIFA World Cup final, in which England defeated West Germany 4-2 in extra time. The stadium also hosted the 2011 UEFA Champions League final, in which Barcelona defeated Manchester United 3-1.

Another iconic football stadium is the Maracanã Stadium in Rio de Janeiro, Brazil. The stadium was built in 1950 for the FIFA World Cup, and it has since become one of the most important football venues in South America. The Maracanã has hosted several important matches, including the 1950 World Cup final between Brazil and Uruguay. The stadium was also used for the opening and closing ceremonies of the 2016 Olympic Games in Rio de Janeiro.

In the United States, one of the most iconic football stadiums is Lambeau Field in Green Bay, Wisconsin. Lambeau Field has been the home of the Green Bay Packers since 1957, and it is one of the oldest stadiums in the NFL. The stadium is known for its cold weather and raucous crowds, and it has become a symbol of the Packers' success on the football field.

Another iconic football stadium in the United States is the Rose Bowl in Pasadena, California. The Rose Bowl has been the site of the Rose Bowl Game, one of the most prestigious college football bowl games, since 1923. The stadium has also hosted several important international soccer matches, including the 1994 FIFA World Cup final between Brazil and Italy.

In Europe, one of the most historic football stadiums is Camp Nou in Barcelona, Spain. Camp Nou has been the home of FC Barcelona since 1957, and it is the largest football stadium in Europe, with a seating capacity of over 99,000. The stadium has hosted several important football matches, including the final of the 1999 UEFA Champions League, in which Manchester United defeated Bayern Munich 2-1 in stoppage time.

Another historic football stadium in Europe is Old Trafford in Manchester, England. Old Trafford has been the home of Manchester United since 1910, and it is one of the most iconic football stadiums in the world. The stadium has hosted several important matches, including the 1966 FIFA World Cup final, in which England defeated West Germany 4-2 in extra time. Old Trafford has also hosted several important international club matches, including the 2003 UEFA Champions League final between AC Milan and Juventus.

In South America, one of the most historic football stadiums is La Bombonera in Buenos Aires, Argentina. La Bombonera has been the home of Boca Juniors since 1940, and it is one of the most intimidating stadiums in the world for opposing teams. The stadium is known for its steep stands, which give fans an excellent view of the action on the field. La Bombonera has hosted several important matches, including the 1978 FIFA World Cup final between Argentina and the Netherlands.

In Africa, one of the most iconic football stadiums is the Soccer City Stadium in Johannesburg, South Africa. The stadium was built for the 2010 FIFA World Cup, and it has a seating capacity of over 94,000. The stadium hosted the opening and closing ceremonies of the 2010 World Cup, as well as the final between Spain and the Netherlands.

Modern marvels

Football stadiums have come a long way since the early days of the sport. Today, stadiums are more than just a place to watch a game. They are architectural wonders and engineering feats, boasting modern technology and amenities that enhance the overall experience for fans.

One of the most iconic modern football stadiums is the AT&T Stadium in Arlington, Texas, home of the Dallas Cowboys. Opened in 2009, the stadium boasts a retractable roof, a massive video screen that spans from one 20-yard line to the other, and a seating capacity of over 100,000. The stadium is also known for its massive doors, which can be opened to allow for natural ventilation and a view of the surrounding area.

Another impressive modern stadium is Mercedes-Benz Stadium in Atlanta, Georgia, which opened in 2017. The stadium features a retractable roof that opens like a camera lens, and a giant, circular video board that surrounds the interior of the roof. The stadium is also known for its sustainable design, including a rainwater collection system and energy-efficient lighting.

In addition to modern marvels, there are also several historic football stadiums that hold a special place in the hearts of fans. One such stadium is Lambeau Field in Green Bay, Wisconsin, home of the Green Bay Packers. Opened in 1957, the stadium has undergone several renovations over the years, but still maintains its classic feel and charm. The stadium is also known for its "frozen tundra," a reference to the often cold and snowy conditions of the late-season games played there.

Another historic stadium is Notre Dame Stadium in South Bend, Indiana, home of the Notre Dame Fighting Irish. The stadium opened in 1930 and has undergone several renovations over the years. The stadium is known for its iconic "Touchdown Jesus" mural, which depicts a larger-than-life Jesus with his arms outstretched, and its capacity of over 77,000.

Aside from football-specific stadiums, some of the most iconic venues for the sport include college and professional stadiums that are also used for other purposes. For example, the Rose Bowl in Pasadena, California, is a multi-purpose stadium that has hosted football games, concerts, and even the 1994 FIFA World Cup. Similarly, the Los Angeles Memorial Coliseum has hosted everything from football games to the 1984 Summer Olympics.

One of the unique aspects of football stadiums is the role they play in the community. Not only do they serve as a gathering place for fans on game days, but they can also be used for other events, such as concerts, festivals, and even religious services. Additionally, they can bring economic benefits to the surrounding area, as fans flock to the stadium and spend money on food, merchandise, and local businesses.

Overall, football stadiums have evolved from simple, utilitarian structures to stunning feats of architecture and technology. Whether it's a historic stadium with a classic feel, or a modern marvel with all the latest amenities, football stadiums hold a special place in the hearts of fans and communities around the world.

The college football gameday experience

The college football gameday experience is a unique and cherished tradition in American sports. Every weekend during the fall, thousands of fans gather on college campuses across the country to watch their favorite teams play. From tailgating to marching bands to student sections, the gameday atmosphere is something that cannot be replicated in any other sport.

The day usually starts early with fans arriving hours before kickoff to set up their tailgate parties. Grills are fired up, coolers are stocked with beverages, and tents and chairs are set up to create the perfect pre-game party atmosphere. Fans often wear team colors and dress up in creative outfits to show their spirit and support for their team.

One of the most iconic parts of the college football gameday experience is the marching band. These bands are an integral part of the game and bring energy and excitement to the stadium. They perform a variety of songs and routines, including the team fight song, halftime shows, and fan favorites. Many of these bands have become famous in their own right, such as Ohio State's "TBDBITL" (The Best Damn Band in the Land) and the University of Michigan's "The Victors."

The student section is another important aspect of the gameday experience. These sections are usually located in the end zone or sideline and are reserved for students who want to cheer on their team. They are known for their creative and rowdy behavior, including chants, dances, and crowd-surfing. The student section creates an atmosphere of excitement and energy that is contagious throughout the stadium.

When it comes time for the game, fans file into the stadium and find their seats. The atmosphere is electric as the teams take the field and the crowd erupts into cheers. The game itself is a spectacle of athletic prowess, with players showcasing their skills in running, passing, and tackling. The excitement builds as the game progresses, and fans eagerly cheer on their team to victory.

Halftime is another important part of the gameday experience. This is when the marching band takes center stage and performs their halftime show. Fans often take the opportunity to grab a snack or visit the restroom during this time, but many stay to watch the performance.

As the game draws to a close, the tension builds as fans root for their team to secure a victory. If the game is close, the energy in the stadium reaches a fever pitch as every play becomes crucial. When the game ends, the winning team celebrates while the losing team and their fans head back to their tailgates, disappointed but already looking forward to the next game.

The college football gameday experience is more than just a sporting event; it is a celebration of school spirit, tradition, and community. It brings together people from all walks of life, united in their love of the game and their support for their team. From the pre-game tailgate parties to the post-game celebrations, the gameday experience is an unforgettable experience that has captured the hearts of sports fans across the country.

Football Equipment and Gear

Football is a physical sport that requires players to wear specific equipment and gear to ensure their safety and enhance their performance on the field. Over the years, the design and technology of football equipment have evolved, leading to improved safety and performance for players. Below we will we will discuss the various types of equipment and gear used in football, their importance, and how they have evolved over time.

Helmets are the most crucial piece of equipment in football. They protect the player's head and brain from the impact of collisions during a game. The earliest football helmets were made of leather and lacked any form of padding or protection. However, the modern football helmet is made up of a hard outer shell and an inner padding system that helps to absorb the force of collisions. The helmets are also fitted with a face mask that protects the player's face from impacts and collisions. Helmets are tested to ensure that they meet safety standards before they are sold or used in a game.

The shoulder pads are another important piece of equipment that is worn by players in football. They are designed to protect the player's shoulders, chest, and back from collisions. The earliest shoulder pads were made of leather, but modern pads are made of foam padding and hard plastic. The pads are designed to be light, flexible, and durable, allowing players to move freely and comfortably while also providing adequate protection.

Football players also wear gloves to improve their grip on the ball, especially when it is wet or slippery. The gloves are made of synthetic materials that provide a tacky surface that helps players hold onto the ball. In recent years, gloves have become more specialized, with some gloves designed specifically for receivers or quarterbacks. These gloves provide a better grip, flexibility, and durability, which allows players to catch or throw the ball more efficiently.

Cleats are another essential piece of equipment in football. They provide players with the necessary traction and support to move and change direction quickly on the field. The earliest football cleats were made of leather with metal studs. However, modern cleats are made of synthetic materials and have molded plastic or rubber studs. The studs are designed to provide different types of traction for different playing surfaces, such as grass, turf, or indoor courts.

Apart from the essential equipment and gear, football players also wear various accessories that help to enhance their performance on the field. Mouthguards are worn to protect the player's teeth and jaw from impacts, while thigh and knee pads are used to protect the player's legs from collisions. Neck rolls are also worn by some players to protect their necks and spine from impacts.

Over the years, the design and technology of football equipment and gear have evolved to improve player safety and performance. For example, the NFL implemented new helmet safety rules that require players to use helmets that meet specific safety standards. The new rules also prohibit players from using helmets that are more than ten years old. Additionally, the design of helmets has improved to provide better protection against concussions and other head injuries.

Shoulder pads have also evolved over time, with manufacturers incorporating new materials and designs that provide better protection and comfort. For instance, some shoulder pads are now made with shock-absorbing materials that reduce the impact of collisions. Gloves have also undergone significant changes, with manufacturers developing new materials and designs that provide better grip and flexibility.

Protective equipment and its evolution

Protective equipment has been a critical component of football since its inception, and over time, this gear has evolved to provide players with more comprehensive protection. Initially, players wore minimal equipment that consisted mainly of leather helmets and pads, but as the game became more physical, the gear became more advanced. Below we will we will explore the history and evolution of football equipment and gear, including helmets, shoulder pads, cleats, and other protective gear.

Helmets are one of the most critical pieces of equipment in football, providing vital protection for the head and brain. Early helmets were simple leather caps that offered little protection from collisions, and players still suffered severe head injuries. In 1939, Riddell introduced the first plastic helmet, which was a significant improvement in protection. Over time, helmets have continued to evolve, with manufacturers adding additional padding, improving ventilation, and introducing new materials. The most significant advancements in helmet technology came in the 21st century, with the introduction of helmets that could measure impacts and alert sideline staff if a player sustained a significant blow to the head.

Shoulder pads are another essential piece of equipment that have undergone significant changes over the years. In the early days of football, players wore minimal shoulder pads that consisted of leather or felt padding. As the game became more physical, pads became more substantial and offered more protection. Today's shoulder pads are made from high-tech materials and are designed to protect players' shoulders, ribs, and chest. These pads have also become more specialized, with linemen wearing thicker and heavier pads than other players to protect against collisions.

Cleats are another crucial piece of equipment for football players, providing traction and stability on the field. In the early days of the game, players wore simple leather shoes with flat soles. As the game became more sophisticated, manufacturers introduced cleats with spikes to provide better traction. Modern cleats are made from lightweight, durable materials and feature various stud configurations designed to provide optimal traction on different types of playing surfaces.

Other protective gear, such as mouthguards, eye shields, and thigh pads, have also evolved over time to provide more comprehensive protection. Mouthguards, for example, were initially optional, but today they are mandatory in most leagues to protect against dental injuries and concussions. Eye shields, which were once an optional accessory, have become a standard feature in many helmets to protect against eye injuries. Thigh pads, which were once optional, are now mandatory in many leagues to protect against thigh contusions and other injuries.

One of the most significant advancements in football equipment in recent years has been the introduction of technology to monitor and track players' performance and health. GPS trackers, for example, can be used to monitor players' movements and provide coaches with data on their speed, distance, and acceleration. Heart rate monitors can be used to track players' exertion levels and ensure they are not overworking themselves. These technologies can also be used to monitor players for signs of dehydration and fatigue, allowing coaches to make more informed decisions about player substitutions.

In addition to advances in equipment technology, there have also been significant changes in the rules governing equipment use. For example, the National Football League (NFL) has implemented strict rules governing helmet use, mandating that players wear only approved helmets that have been independently tested for safety. The NFL has also banned certain types of equipment, such as the use of certain types of facemasks and the use of non-standard equipment modifications.

The role of technology in gear innovation

In the game of football, having the right equipment and gear is crucial to player safety and performance. Over the years, advances in technology have led to significant improvements in the design and functionality of football equipment. From helmets to cleats, every piece of gear has undergone significant changes to provide better protection, comfort, and performance for players.

One of the most significant advancements in football equipment has been the development of the helmet. In the early days of football, players wore leather helmets with little to no protection from hard hits or collisions. As the game evolved and player safety became a more significant concern, helmet design has undergone significant changes.

Modern helmets are designed to absorb and disperse impact forces and protect against head and neck injuries. The development of the chinstrap has also helped to keep the helmet in place during collisions, further reducing the risk of injury. Recently, the introduction of new materials and technologies such as air pads, shock absorbers, and sensors has improved the ability of helmets to protect players from head injuries.

Another crucial piece of protective equipment in football is shoulder pads. The design of shoulder pads has also undergone significant changes over the years, with a focus on reducing weight while still providing adequate protection. The development of new materials such as Kevlar and carbon fiber has helped to make shoulder pads more lightweight, while still providing the necessary protection.

Cleats are another important piece of gear in football, as they provide traction and stability on the playing field. In recent years, advancements in technology have led to the development of cleats with better traction and grip, reducing the risk of slips and falls. The design of cleats has also evolved, with a focus on comfort, durability, and style.

Technology has played a significant role in the innovation of football gear. One of the most significant developments has been the use of 3D printing in the production of football equipment. 3D printing allows for the creation of custom-fit equipment, reducing the risk of injury and increasing comfort for players. It also enables the rapid prototyping of new gear designs, making it easier for manufacturers to test and improve their products.

Another technology that has had a significant impact on football gear is the use of sensors. Sensors can be integrated into helmets and other gear to provide real-time data on the impact of hits and collisions. This data can help coaches and trainers make informed decisions about player safety and help to identify potential injuries before they become more severe.

In addition to technology, the development of football gear has also been influenced by fashion and style. The design of uniforms has evolved over the years, with a focus on creating a distinctive look for each team. Color schemes, logos, and other design elements have become an important part of team identity and fan culture.

Proper fitting and maintenance

Proper fitting and maintenance of football equipment and gear is crucial for the safety and performance of players. Football is a contact sport where players are exposed to physical impact and collisions, making it necessary for them to wear protective gear that is properly fitted and maintained to prevent injuries.

One of the most critical pieces of equipment is the helmet. It protects the head and face from impacts and collisions that could cause concussions, facial injuries, or dental injuries. A properly fitted helmet should fit snugly on the head, with no gaps between the helmet and the player's head. It should also be level on the head, with the chin strap properly secured. A helmet that is too loose or too tight can increase the risk of injury, and players should have their helmets checked for fit and condition regularly.

The shoulder pads are also important protective gear that covers the player's upper body and shoulders. They help absorb the impact of collisions and protect the player's chest, back, and collarbones. Shoulder pads should be properly sized for the player's body, with the top of the pads extending to the base of the neck and the bottom of the pads covering the ribs. The player should be able to move freely with the shoulder pads on, but they should not shift or move during play.

Other protective gear includes thigh pads, hip pads, knee pads, and elbow pads. These pads help protect players from impact and reduce the risk of injury to these areas. They should fit snugly and be properly positioned for maximum protection.

In addition to protective gear, football players also wear specialized equipment for their positions. For example, linemen wear gloves with extra padding and grip to help them grip and control their opponents. Receivers wear gloves with a tacky material that helps them catch the ball more easily. Kickers and punters wear shoes with a specialized sole for better traction on the field.

Proper maintenance of football equipment is also crucial for its longevity and effectiveness. Players should clean their equipment after each practice or game to prevent bacteria buildup and reduce the risk of infection. Helmets should be wiped down with an approved disinfectant, and shoulder pads and other pads should be wiped down with a damp cloth. Equipment should be inspected regularly for any signs of wear or damage and replaced as needed.

In recent years, technology has played a significant role in the development of football equipment. Companies are constantly working to improve the protective qualities of equipment while also making it more lightweight and comfortable for players. For example, helmet technology has advanced to include shock-absorbing materials and sensors that measure the force of impacts. Some helmets also feature specialized ventilation systems to keep players cool during games.

The importance of proper fitting and maintenance of football equipment cannot be overstated. Players who do not wear properly fitted gear or maintain it regularly are at increased risk of injury. In addition, equipment that is not maintained or replaced as needed can lose its protective qualities and increase the risk of injury.

Coaches and trainers should educate their players on the importance of proper equipment fitting and maintenance and check their gear regularly for fit and condition. They should also ensure that players have access to the latest technology and equipment to keep them safe and performing at their best. With proper equipment care and technology, football players can stay safe and protected on the field.

Sportsmanship and Team Building

Sportsmanship and team building are two of the most critical aspects of football. Football is not just about winning games, but it is also about developing young athletes into well-rounded individuals who know the importance of teamwork, sportsmanship, and respect. Below we will we will explore the importance of sportsmanship and team building in football.

Sportsmanship is a critical aspect of football. The game of football is not just about winning and losing; it is also about how players conduct themselves on the field. Good sportsmanship is about respecting your opponent, your teammates, and the rules of the game. When players display good sportsmanship, they show that they understand the value of teamwork, respect, and fairness. Good sportsmanship is also important for building character and developing young athletes into responsible individuals who will go on to make a positive contribution to society.

One of the most significant aspects of sportsmanship in football is fair play. Football is a game of rules, and it is essential that players understand and respect these rules. Players must learn to accept the decisions made by officials and referees, even if they do not always agree with them. This includes avoiding any forms of cheating or unsportsmanlike behavior, such as diving, time-wasting, or using abusive language.

Another important aspect of sportsmanship is respect. Players must respect their opponents and teammates, as well as the coaches, officials, and spectators. Players must also respect the game of football itself, and the traditions and values it represents. This includes showing respect for the opposing team's equipment and property, as well as for the field of play.

Team building is another essential aspect of football. Football is a team sport, and success depends on how well the team works together. Effective team building involves developing a sense of unity, purpose, and commitment among the players. This requires a strong sense of leadership from the coaches and the senior players, as well as a willingness to work together and support each other.

One of the most important aspects of team building is communication. Players must learn to communicate effectively with each other, both on and off the field. This means understanding each other's strengths and weaknesses, and developing a game plan that takes advantage of these strengths while minimizing the weaknesses. Effective communication also involves being able to give and receive feedback, and being willing to learn from mistakes and make improvements.

Another important aspect of team building is trust. Players must learn to trust each other, and to trust the coaches and the team's system of play. This involves developing a sense of shared responsibility and accountability, and a willingness to work hard and sacrifice for the team's success. Players must also learn to trust their instincts and make quick decisions, without second-guessing themselves or their teammates.

Leadership is also an important aspect of team building. Effective leaders set a positive example for their teammates, both on and off the field. They lead by example, demonstrating a strong work ethic, a positive attitude, and a willingness to take responsibility for their actions. They also help to build team cohesion by creating a sense of purpose and a shared vision for the team's success.

The importance of teamwork

Teamwork is an essential aspect of any team sport, and football is no exception. A football team comprises of 11 players, each with a specific role and responsibility to ensure that the team performs to its best potential. However, the team's success is not only based on individual skills but also on the players' ability to work together as a unit. Below we will we will discuss the importance of teamwork in football and how it can lead to success on and off the field.

The first and most crucial aspect of teamwork is communication. Communication between players is essential to ensure that everyone is on the same page and knows what their role is in a particular play. Football is a fast-paced game, and players need to communicate quickly and efficiently to make split-second decisions. This communication can happen through various means, such as verbal cues, hand signals, or pre-designed plays. The quarterback is often the leader of the team and needs to communicate effectively with the other players to ensure that the team can execute plays correctly.

Another aspect of teamwork is trust. Trust is built over time and comes from players knowing that their teammates can execute their assigned roles effectively. Each player must know and trust that their teammate will do their job to the best of their ability. When players trust each other, they can work together with greater efficiency and effectiveness, leading to better results on the field.

In football, each player has a specific role to play, and it is essential that they understand and perform their duties to the best of their abilities. A player who doesn't execute their role can cause the entire play to fail, leading to poor results. Therefore, it is crucial that each player understands the importance of their role and executes it effectively. When every player performs their role to the best of their ability, the team can achieve its goals and succeed on the field.

Teamwork also plays a vital role in building team morale and spirit. When players work together to achieve a common goal, they build a sense of camaraderie that is essential for a team's success. This camaraderie can lead to increased motivation, better communication, and a willingness to work together to achieve success. A positive team spirit can help players overcome challenges and push themselves to achieve greater things on and off the field.

Football is a sport that requires a high degree of physical fitness and conditioning. The rigorous training sessions, practices, and games can take a toll on players' bodies and minds. Therefore, it is crucial to have a supportive team environment that can provide players with the emotional support they need to perform at their best. A positive team environment can help players cope with the physical and emotional challenges of the sport, leading to better results on the field.

Another important aspect of teamwork in football is the ability to adapt to changing situations. Football games are unpredictable, and teams need to be able to adapt to changing circumstances quickly. Teams need to be flexible and adjust their game plans based on the opponents' strengths and weaknesses. Players need to be able to make adjustments on the fly and work together to execute new strategies effectively.

Finally, teamwork in football extends beyond the field. Players need to be able to work together off the field to build lasting relationships that can help them succeed both in and out of the sport. This can include activities such as team-building exercises, community service projects, or simply spending time together as a team. Building these relationships can help players develop a deeper sense of connection and trust with their teammates, leading to better results on the field.

Building team chemistry

Building team chemistry is a crucial aspect of any successful football team. It refers to the relationship between players and how they work together on and off the field. A team with strong chemistry can perform at a higher level, be more resilient in tough situations, and build a positive team culture that lasts for years. Below we will we will discuss the importance of building team chemistry and the strategies that coaches can use to foster a cohesive team environment.

The first step in building team chemistry is to establish a positive team culture. This begins with the coach setting the tone for the team and establishing clear expectations for behavior both on and off the field. Coaches should emphasize the importance of teamwork and respect, and encourage players to support one another. This can be achieved through team-building activities, such as group dinners, team outings, and community service projects.

Another important aspect of building team chemistry is communication. Players need to feel comfortable communicating with one another and with their coaches. This includes both on-field communication during games and practices, as well as off-field communication through regular team meetings and one-on-one conversations. Coaches should create a safe space for players to voice their concerns and ideas, and encourage players to support each other through positive feedback and constructive criticism.

Trust is another essential component of team chemistry. Players need to trust one another both on and off the field. This includes trusting their teammates to execute their responsibilities on the field, as well as trusting them to be reliable and supportive off the field. Coaches can help build trust by encouraging players to work together and by recognizing and rewarding teamwork.

Building team chemistry also involves embracing diversity. Teams are made up of individuals with unique backgrounds, personalities, and skillsets. Coaches should encourage players to appreciate and learn from one another's differences, and create an inclusive team culture that celebrates diversity.

Finally, building team chemistry requires a commitment to ongoing improvement. Coaches should encourage players to continuously strive to be better, both individually and as a team. This involves setting goals and tracking progress, as well as regularly evaluating and adjusting the team's strategies and tactics.

In conclusion, building team chemistry is a crucial aspect of any successful football team. Coaches can foster a cohesive team environment by establishing a positive team culture, encouraging communication, building trust, embracing diversity, and committing to ongoing improvement. By focusing on these strategies, coaches can create a team that is resilient, supportive, and capable of achieving its goals.

Lessons from football for life

Football is a sport that not only provides physical fitness but also teaches valuable lessons that can be applied in life. From teamwork and dedication to overcoming adversity, the skills and values learned on the football field can translate to success in various aspects of life. Below we will we will discuss some of the important life lessons that can be learned from football.

Teamwork is the foundation of football, and it is essential for success on the field. Each player has a specific role to play, and the success of the team depends on each player fulfilling their responsibilities. The same can be applied to life. Whether it's in the workplace or in personal relationships, success is often dependent on the ability to work effectively with others. The lessons learned from playing football can help individuals become better team players and learn how to collaborate with others to achieve a common goal.

Another important lesson that can be learned from football is dedication. Football is a physically demanding sport that requires a great deal of time and effort to master. Players must be dedicated to their training and put in hours of practice to hone their skills. This dedication can be applied to other areas of life as well. Whether it's in academics or career, dedication is crucial for success. By dedicating oneself to a task, one can become an expert in their field and achieve their goals.

Overcoming adversity is another important lesson that can be learned from football. Injuries, losing streaks, and other challenges are inevitable in football. Players must learn how to overcome these challenges and bounce back from setbacks. The same can be applied to life. Life is full of challenges and setbacks, and the ability to overcome adversity is essential for success. Football can teach individuals how to develop a resilient mindset and bounce back from failure.

Leadership is also an important lesson that can be learned from football. Football teams often have team captains or other leaders who are responsible for guiding and motivating their teammates. These leaders must set an example for their teammates and be able to inspire them to perform at their best. This leadership can be applied to other areas of life as well. Whether it's in the workplace or in personal relationships, leadership skills are essential for success. Football can teach individuals how to be effective leaders and inspire others to achieve their goals.

Sportsmanship is another important lesson that can be learned from football. Football is a competitive sport, and players must learn how to compete while maintaining respect for their opponents. This can be applied to life as well. In both personal and professional settings, it is important to compete ethically and maintain a level of respect for others. Football can teach individuals how to be competitive while maintaining their integrity and sportsmanship.

In conclusion, football is a sport that teaches valuable lessons that can be applied in various aspects of life. From teamwork and dedication to overcoming adversity and leadership, the skills and values learned on the football field can translate to success in other areas of life. Whether it's in the workplace or in personal relationships, the lessons learned from football can help individuals become better team players, leaders, and overall successful individuals.

High School Football

High school football is a beloved American tradition that has been around for more than a century. It's a sport that brings communities together and helps instill values such as teamwork, discipline, and dedication. Below we will examine the history and importance of high school football, the challenges it faces, and its impact on young athletes.

The history of high school football dates back to the late 19th century when the sport was gaining popularity at the college level. By the turn of the century, high schools began to form their teams, and football quickly became a staple of American high school sports. In the years that followed, high school football grew in popularity, and today it remains one of the most popular sports in the United States.

High school football is not just a sport, but it's also a way for young athletes to learn important life skills. Teamwork is one of the most critical lessons that high school football teaches. Players learn to work together to achieve a common goal, and they develop a sense of camaraderie that can last a lifetime. They also learn about discipline, hard work, and dedication, which can help them succeed in other areas of their lives.

Playing high school football is also a great way to develop physical fitness. Football is a physically demanding sport that requires strength, speed, and agility. Through rigorous training and practice, players can improve their physical abilities, which can help them in other sports and in their daily lives.

However, high school football is not without its challenges. One of the biggest challenges facing high school football is the risk of injury. Football is a contact sport that can lead to serious injuries such as concussions, broken bones, and torn ligaments. In recent years, there has been a growing concern over the safety of high school football, and many schools and organizations have taken steps to make the sport safer for young athletes.

Another challenge facing high school football is the cost. Football is an expensive sport that requires a lot of equipment and facilities. Schools must invest in high-quality equipment, facilities, and coaching staff to provide their athletes with the best possible experience. For many schools, the cost of providing a football program can be a significant financial burden.

Despite these challenges, high school football remains an important part of American culture. It's a sport that brings communities together, and it provides young athletes with valuable life lessons. High school football players often become leaders in their communities and go on to achieve great success in their lives.

In conclusion, high school football is a beloved American tradition that has been around for more than a century. It's a sport that teaches important life skills such as teamwork, discipline, and dedication. Although high school football faces challenges such as the risk of injury and the cost of equipment, it remains an important part of American culture and will continue to be a beloved sport for generations to come.

The role of high school football in communities

High school football is a significant part of American culture. The sport provides students with an opportunity to showcase their talents and compete against other schools in their region. It is an excellent way for young athletes to learn about teamwork, discipline, and dedication while fostering a sense of community pride. Below we will explore the role of high school football in communities and the impact it has on students, fans, and the community.

One of the primary benefits of high school football is that it provides an opportunity for students to develop valuable life skills. Football is a team sport that requires cooperation, communication, and trust. These skills are essential for success both on and off the field. In addition, football teaches discipline, hard work, and perseverance. It takes time, effort, and dedication to excel in football, and these same traits can be applied to other areas of life, such as academics and career development.

High school football also fosters a sense of community pride. When a high school football team wins a game, it is not just a victory for the team but for the entire community. It brings people together and creates a sense of unity and shared purpose. This is particularly true in smaller communities where the high school football team is often the center of attention on Friday nights during the season.

Another way high school football benefits communities is by generating revenue for local businesses. Football games bring people into the community, and they often spend money on food, drinks, and other items while attending the game. This can be a significant boost to the local economy, particularly in small towns where there may be fewer businesses.

High school football also provides a source of entertainment for fans. Many people look forward to attending football games on Friday nights, and it is an opportunity to socialize with friends and family while cheering on the local team. This sense of community and camaraderie is a significant part of the high school football experience.

While high school football has many benefits, there are also some concerns that need to be addressed. One of the biggest concerns is player safety. Football is a contact sport, and players are at risk of injury, particularly head injuries. Schools and communities need to ensure that they are taking appropriate measures to protect players, such as providing proper equipment, coaching, and medical attention.

Another concern is the cost of high school football programs. Football programs require significant resources, including coaching staff, equipment, and facilities. Schools and communities need to ensure that they are allocating resources appropriately to ensure that other programs and services are not being overlooked or underfunded.

In conclusion, high school football plays an essential role in communities across America. It provides students with an opportunity to develop valuable life skills, fosters a sense of community pride, and generates revenue for local businesses. However, it is essential to address concerns such as player safety and program costs to ensure that high school football remains a positive experience for all involved.

Developing talent and preparing for college

High school football is an important part of the American sporting landscape. It is a time when young athletes can showcase their skills, develop their talent, and prepare for the next level of competition. Beyond the competitive aspect of the game, high school football plays a crucial role in the development of young people, teaching important lessons about teamwork, leadership, and hard work.

For many high school athletes, football is a way of life. They devote countless hours to training, studying game film, and preparing for competition. These efforts are often rewarded with the opportunity to compete against other schools in front of their friends, family, and community. This sense of pride and belonging is a key reason why high school football is such an important part of American culture.

But high school football is not just about winning games. It is also a place where young people can learn important life skills that will serve them well beyond the gridiron. One of the most important of these skills is teamwork. Football is a team sport, and success on the field requires each player to work together towards a common goal. In order to win, players must learn to trust one another, communicate effectively, and put the needs of the team ahead of their own individual goals. These lessons can be applied to all aspects of life, from the classroom to the workplace.

In addition to teamwork, high school football teaches valuable lessons about leadership. Captains and other team leaders must set an example for their teammates, both on and off the field. They must motivate their teammates, hold them accountable, and provide guidance when necessary. These skills are essential for success in any area of life, from business to politics.

Another important aspect of high school football is the opportunity for personal growth and development. Athletes must push themselves physically and mentally in order to perform at their best. They must learn to overcome adversity, whether it be a tough opponent or a personal setback. This resilience and determination will serve them well throughout their lives.

Of course, high school football is not without its challenges. One of the biggest issues facing the sport is the risk of injury. Football is a contact sport, and players are at risk of serious injury every time they take the field. This risk has led to increased attention on player safety, with many schools implementing new rules and protocols to protect their athletes. This includes everything from limiting contact during practice to providing better equipment and medical care.

Despite these challenges, high school football remains an important part of American culture. It provides young athletes with the opportunity to develop their skills, learn important life lessons, and be a part of something bigger than themselves. As the sport continues to evolve, it is important that we continue to prioritize the safety and well-being of our young athletes, while also celebrating the unique traditions and culture of high school football.

Legendary high school programs and coaches

High school football has long been an important part of American sports culture. In many parts of the country, it is a way of life and a community-wide event every Friday night in the fall. From the largest cities to the smallest towns, high school football brings people together and provides a sense of pride and identity for the local community. Below we will we will explore some of the legendary high school football programs and coaches who have left their mark on the sport.

One of the most well-known high school football programs in the country is the De La Salle Spartans from Concord, California. The team has a record-setting 151-game winning streak from 1992 to 2003, which is still the longest in high school football history. During that span, they won 12 state championships and several national titles. The team's success was due in large part to head coach Bob Ladouceur, who led the program from 1979 to 2012. Ladouceur's coaching philosophy focused on discipline, hard work, and teamwork, and he emphasized the importance of character and values over winning at all costs.

Another legendary high school football program is the Southlake Carroll Dragons from Southlake, Texas. The team has won eight state championships and produced several NFL players, including Chase Daniel, Greg McElroy, and Riley Dodge. The program's success is due in part to head coach Todd Dodge, who led the team from 2000 to 2006 and then returned in 2014. Dodge's offensive system, known as the "Air Raid," helped the team win four state championships and set numerous offensive records. He also emphasized the importance of building a strong culture and creating a family atmosphere within the team.

In Florida, the Miami Northwestern Bulls have long been one of the top high school football programs in the state. The team has won six state championships and produced several NFL players, including Teddy Bridgewater, Amari Cooper, and Lavonte David. Head coach Eddie "The Magician" Brown led the team to four state championships from 2006 to 2011 and emphasized the importance of hard work, discipline, and family. Brown was known for his innovative offensive schemes and his ability to develop talent, and he has been recognized as one of the top high school coaches in the country.

In Ohio, the Massillon Tigers have a storied football history dating back to the early 1900s. The team has won 24 state championships and produced several NFL players, including Paul Brown, Chris Spielman, and Justin Zwick. The program's success is due in part to head coach Paul Brown, who led the team from 1932 to 1940 and developed several innovative offensive schemes that are still used in football today. Brown later went on to become a legendary NFL coach and helped found the Cleveland Browns franchise.

Finally, in Alabama, the Hoover Buccaneers have established themselves as one of the top high school football programs in the country. The team has won 12 state championships and produced several NFL players, including Marlon Humphrey, Josh Chapman, and Ross Wilson. The program's success is due in part to head coach Rush Propst, who led the team from 1999 to 2007 and emphasized the importance of discipline, hard work, and attention to detail. Propst later went on to coach at other high schools in the state and was the subject of the popular reality TV show "Two-A-Days."

These are just a few examples of the many legendary high school football programs and coaches who have left their mark on the sport. These programs and coaches have not only achieved great success on the field but have also helped develop young men into responsible and productive members of society.

Inspirational Stories

Inspirational stories are a powerful tool for motivating and inspiring individuals to achieve their goals. Football has been the backdrop for many inspiring stories, showcasing the resilience, dedication, and perseverance required to succeed in the sport. These stories range from players overcoming physical limitations to teams overcoming seemingly insurmountable odds to win championships. Here are just a few examples of some of the most inspirational football stories.

One of the most famous inspirational football stories is that of Jim Abbott, a pitcher in Major League Baseball. Abbott was born without a right hand, but that didn't stop him from pursuing his dream of playing professional sports. He excelled in football in high school, playing quarterback and leading his team to the state championship game. He then went on to play college football at the University of Michigan, where he was a starting pitcher on the baseball team as well. In 1987, he was drafted by the California Angels and went on to have a successful career, including throwing a no-hitter in 1993.

Another inspiring story comes from former NFL player, Michael Oher. Oher's life was chronicled in the book and movie, "The Blind Side." Oher grew up in poverty and was in and out of foster care before being taken in by the Tuohy family. With their support, he excelled in football and went on to play in college at the University of Mississippi. In 2009, he was drafted by the Baltimore Ravens and went on to play in the Super Bowl in 2013 as a member of the San Francisco 49ers.

The story of the 2006 Texas Longhorns football team is another inspiring tale. The team was led by quarterback Vince Young, who overcame a difficult childhood to become one of the best players in college football. The Longhorns went undefeated that season and faced off against the heavily favored USC Trojans in the BCS National Championship game. Young put on a show, rushing for 200 yards and three touchdowns and passing for 267 yards and another score. His final touchdown run with 19 seconds left sealed the victory for the Longhorns, and he was named the game's MVP.

The story of Rudy Ruettiger is perhaps one of the most famous inspirational football stories of all time. Ruettiger was a walk-on at Notre Dame in the 1970s and faced numerous obstacles in his quest to make the team. He was undersized and lacked the natural talent of many of his teammates. However, he persevered and finally earned a spot on the roster. In his final game, he was put in for a single play and sacked the opposing quarterback. His story was later turned into a movie, "Rudy," which has become a classic sports film.

Finally, the story of former NFL player, Devon Still, is a heartwarming tale of love and perseverance. Still's daughter, Leah, was diagnosed with cancer in 2014, and he put his NFL career on hold to be with her during her treatments. The Cincinnati Bengals signed him to their practice squad so that he could continue to have health insurance for Leah's treatments. The team later promoted him to the active roster, and he went on to have a successful season. More importantly, Leah beat cancer and became an inspiration to millions of people.

These are just a few of the countless inspirational football stories that exist. From players overcoming physical limitations to teams rallying together to achieve greatness, football has provided us with countless tales of perseverance, dedication, and the human spirit. These stories serve as a reminder of the power of the human will to overcome adversity and achieve greatness.

Overcoming adversity

Overcoming adversity is a common theme in sports, and football is no exception. Many players have had to overcome significant obstacles to achieve success on and off the field. These stories of resilience and determination serve as an inspiration to fans and players alike. Below we will we will explore some of the most inspiring stories of football players who have overcome adversity.

One of the most famous examples of overcoming adversity in football is the story of Michael Oher. Oher was a highly recruited high school football player who was taken in by a wealthy family after he was found wandering the streets. Despite his athletic abilities, Oher struggled academically and had to overcome a learning disability to succeed. He eventually earned a scholarship to play football at the University of Mississippi and was drafted by the Baltimore Ravens in the first round of the 2009 NFL Draft. Oher's story was later adapted into the movie "The Blind Side," which earned an Academy Award for Best Picture.

Another inspiring story is that of Eric LeGrand. LeGrand was a standout defensive lineman at Rutgers University and had dreams of playing in the NFL. In 2010, he suffered a spinal cord injury while making a tackle during a game that left him paralyzed from the neck down. Despite the devastating injury, LeGrand remained positive and committed to his rehabilitation. He has since regained some movement in his shoulders and arms and has become an advocate for spinal cord injury research.

Devon Gales is another football player who overcame a serious injury. Gales was a wide receiver at Southern University when he suffered a spinal cord injury during a game against the University of Georgia in 2015. He was left paralyzed from the waist down and faced a long road to recovery. However, Gales remained determined and focused on his rehabilitation. He has since made progress and regained some movement in his legs.

In addition to physical obstacles, some players have had to overcome significant personal challenges. Maurice Clarett is a former Ohio State running back who was a star on the field but had a troubled personal life. Clarett struggled with substance abuse and was eventually sentenced to prison for armed robbery. However, he was able to turn his life around and now works as a motivational speaker and entrepreneur.

Another example is that of Tim Tebow. Tebow was a Heisman Trophy-winning quarterback at the University of Florida and was selected in the first round of the 2010 NFL Draft. However, he struggled to find success as a starting quarterback in the NFL and was eventually cut by several teams. Despite these setbacks, Tebow remained positive and committed to his faith. He has since found success as a professional baseball player and continues to inspire others with his positive attitude and work ethic.

Finally, the story of Kurt Warner is one of the most inspiring in football history. Warner went undrafted out of college and struggled to make it as a professional football player. He spent several years playing in the Arena Football League and NFL Europe before finally getting a chance to play in the NFL. Warner led the St. Louis Rams to a Super Bowl victory in 1999 and was named the game's MVP. He went on to have a successful career and is now a member of the Pro Football Hall of Fame.

In conclusion, football has produced many inspiring stories of players who have overcome adversity. These stories serve as a reminder that with hard work and determination, anything is possible. Whether it's overcoming physical obstacles or personal challenges, these players have shown that resilience and perseverance can lead to success on and off the field. Their stories serve as an inspiration to fans and players alike and remind us of the power of the human spirit.

Breakthrough performances

Breakthrough performances are an integral part of any sport, and football is no exception. A breakthrough performance can be defined as an individual or team performance that is unexpected, surpasses expectations, and has a significant impact on the outcome of a game or season. These performances can be made by players who have been relatively unknown, or by established players who have been struggling to find their form.

Breakthrough performances can be the result of many factors, including hard work, talent, and opportunity. Some players may have been overlooked by coaches or scouts due to their size, speed, or other physical attributes, but have been able to overcome these obstacles through their determination and work ethic. Other players may have been hindered by injuries or personal issues, but have been able to bounce back and make a significant impact on their team.

One of the most famous breakthrough performances in football history was that of Joe Montana in Super Bowl XXIII. Montana, a quarterback for the San Francisco 49ers, had already established himself as one of the game's greatest players, but his performance in the Super Bowl that year was particularly outstanding. Facing a 16-13 deficit with just over three minutes remaining, Montana led the 49ers on a 92-yard drive that culminated in a touchdown pass to John Taylor with just 34 seconds remaining, giving the 49ers a 20-16 victory. Montana was named the game's Most Valuable Player, and his performance is still considered one of the greatest in Super Bowl history.

Another memorable breakthrough performance was made by David Tyree in Super Bowl XLII. Tyree, a wide receiver for the New York Giants, had been a relatively unknown player throughout his career, but he made a huge impact in the biggest game of his life. With just over a minute remaining and the Giants trailing the undefeated New England Patriots 14-10, Tyree made an incredible catch while being tightly covered by Patriots safety Rodney Harrison. Tyree's helmet catch, as it became known, allowed the Giants to keep their drive alive, and they went on to score the game-winning touchdown a few plays later. Tyree's catch has been called one of the greatest plays in Super Bowl history, and it helped the Giants to secure one of the biggest upsets in NFL history.

Breakthrough performances can also occur at the collegiate level. In 2007, Tim Tebow, a sophomore quarterback for the University of Florida, had already established himself as a talented player, but his performance in the BCS National Championship Game that year was particularly outstanding. Tebow led the Gators to a 41-14 victory over the heavily favored Ohio State Buckeyes, throwing for 231 yards and two touchdowns and rushing for 109 yards and another score. Tebow's performance was a key factor in Florida's victory, and he was named the game's Most Valuable Player.

In addition to individual breakthrough performances, teams can also experience breakthrough seasons. In 2019, the Baltimore Ravens had a breakthrough season, finishing with a league-best record of 14-2 and earning the top seed in the AFC playoffs. Led by quarterback Lamar Jackson, who had a breakout season of his own, the Ravens' high-powered offense and stingy defense made them one of the most dominant teams in the league. Though they were upset by the Tennessee Titans in the divisional round of the playoffs, the Ravens' breakthrough season was a significant accomplishment for a franchise that had not won a playoff game since 2014.

Breakthrough performances are often remembered for years to come, as they can have a lasting impact on the game and the players involved. They can also serve as inspiration for young players and fans, showing that hard work, dedication, and perseverance can lead to success on the field.

Stories of perseverance and determination

Stories of perseverance and determination are what make sports so inspiring. They remind us that even when the odds are against us, anything is possible with hard work, dedication, and a never-give-up attitude. In football, there are countless stories of players who have faced adversity and overcome it to achieve greatness. Here are just a few examples:

Michael Oher - The Blind Side

Michael Oher's story is well-known, thanks in part to the book and movie that bear his name, "The Blind Side." Oher grew up in poverty and struggled in school due to undiagnosed learning disabilities. He was taken in by the Tuohy family, who helped him turn his life around and eventually become a star offensive lineman at Ole Miss. Oher was drafted by the Baltimore Ravens in 2009 and went on to have a successful career in the NFL.

Jim Abbott - One-Handed Pitcher

Jim Abbott was born without a right hand, but that didn't stop him from pursuing his dream of playing professional baseball. He learned to pitch with his left hand and went on to play for the University of Michigan and Team USA before being drafted by the California Angels in 1988. Abbott played 10 seasons in the majors, winning 87 games and earning a Gold Glove award.

Eric LeGrand - Paralyzed While Playing

Eric LeGrand was a standout defensive lineman at Rutgers University until a devastating injury left him paralyzed from the neck down. Despite this setback, LeGrand has remained an inspiration to others. He has continued to be involved with football, working as a radio analyst for Rutgers games and serving as a motivational speaker. He has also raised funds for spinal cord injury research through his charity, Team LeGrand.

Shaquem Griffin - One-Handed Linebacker

Shaquem Griffin was born with a congenital birth defect that resulted in his left hand being amputated when he was just four years old. Despite this, he became a star linebacker at the University of Central Florida, earning AAC Defensive Player of the Year honors in 2016. Griffin was drafted by the Seattle Seahawks in 2018 and has become known for his speed and tenacity on the field.

Eric Berry - Cancer Survivor

Eric Berry was a star safety at the University of Tennessee before being drafted by the Kansas City Chiefs in 2010. In 2014, he was diagnosed with Hodgkin's lymphoma and underwent chemotherapy. Remarkably, he was able to return to the field the following year and earn All-Pro honors. Berry has since become an advocate for cancer awareness and has started his own foundation to help others battling the disease.

These are just a few examples of the many stories of perseverance and determination in sports. They remind us that no matter what obstacles we may face in life, we can overcome them with hard work and a positive attitude.

Have Questions / Comments?

1

This book was designed to cover as much as possible but I know I have probably missed something, or some new amazing discovery that has just come out.

If you notice something missing or have a question that I failed to answer, please get in touch and let me know. If I can, I will email you an answer and also update the book so others can also benefit from it.

Thanks For Being Awesome :)

Submit Your Questions / Comments At:

---

1. https://xspurts.com/posts/questions

https://xspurts.com/posts/questions

Get Another Book Free

1

We love writing and have produced a huge number of books.

For being one of our amazing readers, we would love to offer you another book we have created, 100% free.

To claim this limited time special offer, simply go to the site below and enter your name and email address.

You will then receive one of my great books, direct to your email account, 100% free!

https://xspurts.com/posts/free-book-offer

1. https://xspurts.com/posts/free-book-offer

Also by Marcus B. Cole

Printed in the USA
CPSIA information can be obtained
at www.ICGtesting.com
LVHW020712161023
761195LV00006B/214